Starting New Churches on *Purpose*

Starting
New Churches
on *Purpose*

Strategies for
the 21st Century

Ron Sylvia

20 Empire Drive
Lake Forest, CA 92630

Dedication

This book is dedicated to the
greatest risk takers I know—*church planters*.
Your faith encourages us all to believe God for the impossible
again. May this book ignite your faith and your calling.

I also dedicate this book to *The Springs*,
you have allowed me to live a dream that most people
never get to experience. Thank you for living God's dream for a
New Testament Church and investing in church planters
around the country.

Finally, I dedicate this book to *Teddi Renea*,
the love of my life and my partner in ministry. You risked
everything to begin The Springs with me. I love you more than
yesterday and less than tomorrow.

CONTENTS

ACKNOWLEDGEMENTS

Thanks to Rick Warren for teaching a new generation of church planters how to start churches on purpose. Your passion is contagious, and the principles you have taught us have changed our lives and leadership!

Thanks to Doug Slaybaugh for investing in me and challenging me to write this book. Your friendship through the years has been a constant source of encouragement to me.

Thanks to Andrew Accardy for allowing me to champion Purpose Driven Church Planting. Thanks for your friendship, and for always being an advocate for purpose driven church planters in America.

Thanks to Susan Goetz and the Purpose Driven® Publishing team for working with me on the final edits of the book.

Finally, thanks to the Lord Jesus Christ for allowing all of us to get in on your dream—the local church. To Your Name be the glory forever and ever!

FOREWORD

Ron Sylvia is an experienced and successful church planter. Ron planted the Church @ The Springs in Ocala, Florida, after attending one of Saddleback's Purpose Driven Church Conferences in 1995—the same year I published *The Purpose Driven Church*. He started The Springs with twenty-one people, and it quickly grew to more than three thousand.

As Ron's church grew, so did Ron's heart for church planting. I was so impressed with Ron's passion and skills that I invited him to teach at our Purpose Driven conferences. Ron has now trained thousands of church planters in the steps necessary to start a healthy congregation.

This book is an extraordinarily practical guide on how you can reach your community through a freshly planted, developing congregation. In my mind, what makes this book particularly valuable and unique is that it takes the insights of an experienced church planter and lays them out in chronological order, creating a two-year map for successfully starting—*and completing*—the process of planting a purpose driven church.

In this book, Ron will guide you toward quickly establishing a foundation that will keep your congregation anchored to the purposes of a New Testament church: worship, membership, maturity, ministry, and missions. If you want to be a successful church planter, then this book is an important addition to your library.

May you serve God's purpose in your generation (Acts 13:36). As you do, you will find him leading you on the greatest adventure of your life!

Your friend,

Rick

Rick Warren
Founding Pastor, Saddleback Church

The Dream
of The Springs

God can do anything, you know—far more
than you could ever imagine or guess or request
in your wildest dreams!

Ephesians 3:20 (MSG)

Orlando was a great place to spend my teenage years. Our family moved there from New York the year after Disney World opened in 1972, so I had a front-row seat to the explosion of a city. Hotels were built at a record pace to accommodate the booming tourism industry. Within a few years, our small airport was replaced by an international airport serving over 26 million passengers each year. Orlando became one of the top vacation spots in the world.

Following the lead of Disney World, other theme parks moved into Orlando: Sea World, Universal Studios, Wet 'n' Wild, MGM Studios, and EPCOT. I knew the parks so well that I became a tour guide for visiting family.

Of all the parks, EPCOT was my least favorite. It lacked the excitement and thrill of the other theme parks. For me, it was too educational and sterile. Walt Disney would have felt the same. EPCOT would have been his greatest disappointment, because it was his greatest dream.

Let me explain. Walt Disney was one of the greatest visionaries of this century. He saw in his mind's eye what others could not even imagine. His dreams became entertainment for my generation and generations to follow. His dreams started with a small, line-drawn mouse and blossomed into an empire with Disneyland in California, followed by the behemoth Disney World in my backyard. Yet, his greatest dreaming took place in EPCOT. Disney said this:

> EPCOT will be an experimental prototype community of tomorrow that will take its cue from the new ideas and new technologies that are now emerging . . . It will be a community of tomorrow that will never be completed, but will always be introducing and testing and demonstrating new materials and systems. It will never cease to be a living blueprint of the future, where people actually live a life they can't find anywhere else in the world.[1]

Disney envisioned a community of people living together, ever evolving in their use of technology to live a life they could not experience anywhere else in the world. EPCOT was literally supposed to be a community of people. Every time I visited EPCOT I never saw anyone *living* there. It was a sterile showcase, not a living community. After Walt Disney died, enthusiasm for his EPCOT dream ebbed. It would cost too much and require too much work to build a living, breathing community. So instead, The Disney executives built a showcase of the future— not a community, for it is easier to build a showcase than a community. In the wake of Disney's death, the executives shelved his dream.

We have done the same thing with Jesus' church. He dreamed of a living, breathing organism—a beautiful body that would be his hands and feet to a dying world—a place where people could actually experience a community they cannot find anywhere else in the world. There is nothing like being part of a community, a band of brothers and sisters that are devoted to one another and committed to the mission of advancing God's Kingdom. In Romans 12:10 (NIV) we are admonished to, *Be devoted to one another in brotherly love. Honor one another above yourselves.* Yet today, some have determined it is easier to build a showcase for saints rather than a community for sinners. Church leaders continue to build opulent weekend showcases that are cold and sterile, and lack the warmth and vibrancy of Jesus. Unfortunately, the showcase mentality has neutralized the church of the living Christ.

It's true, communities take hard work to birth and build. But unlike Walt Disney's dream, God's dream did not die. Every day he dreams of people building Experimental Churches of Tomorrow.

The church of this generation needs to look much different than the church of our fathers' generation.

It is time for us to dream again, to believe in the God who inspired Ephesians 3:20–21 (NIV):

> *Now to him who is able to do immeasurably more than we can ever ask or imagine, according to his power at work within us, to him be glory in the church and in Christ Jesus throughout all generations, for ever and ever!*

The church of this generation needs to look much different than the church of our fathers' generation. Today's church must move outside the walls of the building and invade the community. We must be willing to be a laboratory of sorts, experimenting and testing new methodology with the unchanging message of Christ, continually pushing the limits while holding fast to God's dream for his church. We have the awesome privilege of partnering with the Creator of the universe to birth and grow communities of faith—communities that carry and steward the message of the cross.

These communities have been his strategy from the inception of the church. So, how do you build a church from scratch? Where do you start?

My wife, Teddi and I began our church-building journey unexpectedly. We had been in student ministry for ten years. Content within this sphere of ministry, I had told God I was not interested in being a senior pastor—ever. I loved students. I loved that they were willing to take risks. They challenged the status quo rather than surrendering to it. I could dare them to live in radical commitment to Christ, and they would rise to the challenge. Because of this, I had very little interest in challenging the comfortable adult Christian population.

While sitting in a worship service in June of 1994, God and I began a conversation. God's directive was clearly spoken to my heart, "Ron, I want you to begin a contemporary praise and worship church." If God was talking to me, I needed a lot of confirmation. No sooner had that thought left my heart, when my son, Jared, pulled on my shirt sleeve. He was sitting next to me in church doing what nine-year-olds do in church—drawing. He looked at me and said, "Daddy, I love to hear you preach. I wish I could hear you preach every Sunday." Then he went back to drawing.

Of course, I reminded God I would expect my son to say things like that. Again, I asked for confirmation. He began to back up the confirmation dump truck. I immediately looked across the church and connected eyes with a man I had not seen in a month. He simply smiled and nodded to me. He found me after the service and asked if we could have lunch that week, there was something we had to talk about. Our conversation became the second part of the confirmation. He was leaving to find another church—something more contemporary, a praise and worship church. These words were all too familiar. Following that, my leadership in student ministry was questioned by our pastor. He had been to camp and was not comfortable with the "worship style" we were using. He told me if I continued down this path we would come to a crossroad.

Why all of this out of nowhere? I have noticed that when God is stirring in my life, everything familiar becomes uncomfortable. Everything had been fine until that worship service was interrupted by God.

The confirmations kept coming daily through conversations, Scripture, and conflict. It was clear that God was moving my heart to start a new church! But how? Where? When? With what? Why? I knew absolutely nothing about church starting. In my quiet times, God led me to Psalm 37 (a chapter I would return to again and again in that first year). It confirmed the calling to begin Church @ The Springs, and that calling on my life overshadowed all the questions that constantly flooded my mind. Now there were only two choices: obey or disobey. With fear and excitement, the greatest journey of my life began.

Teddi and I knew nothing of what the next year would hold, but we knew the sound of God's voice. He was leading us into unknown territory, yet I realized that he had been

- - - ➤

Church starting,
. . . is the Extreme
Sport of Ministry!

◄ - - -

preparing me for this journey all my life. Everything I had loved about student ministry—risk taking, coloring outside the lines, thinking outside the box, and reaching a new generation with different methodology—all of this applied to starting a new church.

Church starting, I realized, is the Extreme Sport of Ministry! And I had just signed up for the next jump. We were like first-time bungee jumpers. We had to let go of the safety cage and fly—let go of the past and fly toward the future. Letting go of our past was a painful and difficult experience, because we had woven our faith and family into the fabric of our church.

Leaving our students was like tearing out pieces of our hearts and leaving them behind. I had a successful student ministry with a national reputation in those circles, and a good salary—everything that spelled security. God's calling was to leave all of it and follow him down a path I had never considered. Of course, God knew how much my reputation and financial security meant to me. Although an excruciating lesson, I had to lose them both to start this new journey with him. We resigned our Student Ministry position in October of 1994 and gave up everything.

We liquidated all of our retirement and launched Church @ The Springs on November 13, 1994, with nothing—no salary, no denomination or individuals financially supporting us, no church, no people, and very few friends. It was just Jesus and us, but we quickly realized that was all we needed for this journey.

I still get nervous as I remember those days. We were criticized by some former church members, and many people discouraged us. We were told the "demographics were all wrong in Ocala for a church

> - - - →
> *Don't let your God-given dreams die on your pillow. Wake up and live them!*
> ← - - -

like this." I was told it was "political suicide" to start a church in the same town I served in student ministry. In the first years of The Springs, we were called a cult, I was slandered, and my character was assassinated. But as I sit and write this book, we are eleven years into the journey and have seen over 1,500 people come to Christ and over 2,000 follow Christ in baptism. We have grown from 21 people in our first worship service to over 3,000 in weekend attendance. We have been in fourteen different locations. In July of 2005, we purchased 67.5 acres of land. In January of 2006, we opened our second campus at a local high school. What a ride it has been! I have often thought *what if I had said no to God? What if I had given up in the first year?* I would have missed the greatest adventure of my life.

Walt Disney's dream of a new community was never realized. Many church starters, fueled by dreams, will suffer a similar fate. Don't let your God-given dreams die on your pillow. Wake up and live them! This book will help you not only articulate your church-starting dreams, but help you, through the power of the Holy Spirit, to realize them.

---

[1] Disney, Walt. "Walt Disney Quotes," JustDisney.com. © 2002. *http://www.justdisney.com/walt_disney/index.html*

CHAPTER 1

Purpose Driven— Rediscovering the New Testament Church for the 21st Century

Pioneers go where no one has gone before, and they get to experience the thrill of uncharted territory. They think outside the box, color outside the lines, and are never content with the status quo. Rick Warren is a pioneer. He asks questions of current methodology, while holding fast to biblical theology. With a burning desire to reach a new generation for Christ, Rick started the Purpose Driven Church model with Saddleback Church in Southern California in 1990. Since that time, over 300,000 pastors and church leaders have been trained at a *Purpose Driven Church Conference* somewhere in the world.

The Purpose Driven principles are cross-cultural, cross-denominational, and cross-centered. The message is Christ and him crucified, and the process for life change is simple, understandable, and reproducible. Purpose Driven is the DNA of a biblical church. God's purposes are not new; they have been rediscovered for this generation of church leaders.

This book is built on the principles of *The Purpose Driven Church* by Rick Warren which was written on the foundation of Scripture. Rick Warren writes, "It isn't our job to create the purposes of the church, but to discover them."[1]

If you have not yet read Rick's book, I highly recommended that you read it to fully grasp the definition of a Purpose Driven Church. With the success of *The Purpose Driven Church, The Purpose Driven Life*, and *40 Days of Purpose* campaigns, many churches consider themselves "purpose driven churches." Purpose driven churches come in every size, style, denomination, demographic, and location around the world. They can be found from New York City to Rwanda to house boat churches on the Amazon River.

The Purpose Driven principles are cross-cultural, cross-denominational, and cross-centered.

Aubrey Malphurs, a professor at Dallas Theological Seminary and author of *Advanced Strategic Planning*, writes, "The typical church in North America is like a sailboat without a rudder, drifting aimlessly in the ocean. As if that is not bad enough, the winds of change and the currents of postmodernism are relentlessly blowing and pulling it even further off course."[2] The missing rudder is leading, structuring, teaching, and growing a church on purpose. The church does not need to search for a purpose; God has given her a purpose. *The Purpose Driven Church* has helped hundreds of thousands of churches to rediscover God's purposes for this generation.

Rick defines these purposes in *The Purpose Driven Church,*

> ". . . we concluded that although many passages describe what the church is to be and do, two statements by Jesus summarize it all: the Great Commandment (Matt. 22:37–40) and the Great Commission (Matt. 28:19–20).

*Love the Lord your God with all your heart and
with all your soul and with all your mind. . . . Love
your neighbor as yourself. All the Law and the
Prophets hang on these two commandments.*

Matthew 22:37–40

*Go and make disciples of all nations, baptizing
them in the name of the Father and of the Son and
of the Holy Spirit, and teaching them to obey
everything I have commanded you.*

Matthew 28:19–20

A *purpose-driven* church is committed to fulfilling
all five tasks that Christ ordained for his church
to accomplish.

Purpose #1: Love the Lord with all your heart

The word that describes this purpose is *worship*.
The church exists to worship God.

Purpose #2: Love your neighbor as yourself

The word we use to describe this purpose is *ministry*.
The church exists to minister to people.

Purpose #3: Go and make disciples

This purpose we call *evangelism*. The church exists to
communicate God's Word.

Purpose #4: Baptizing them

Why is baptism so important to warrant inclusion
in Christ's Great Commission? I believe it is because
it symbolizes one of the purposes of the church:
fellowship—identification with the body of Christ.
As Christians we're called to *belong*, not just to *believe*.

Purpose #5: Teaching them to obey

The word we commonly use to refer to this purpose
is *discipleship*. The church exists to edify, or educate,
God's people. Discipleship is the process of helping

people become more like Christ in their thoughts,
feelings, and actions."[3]

There is nothing new about these words: Worship, Ministry,
Evangelism, Fellowship, and Discipleship. What is new is the
simple reproducible process of the Purpose Driven Church.

Many have seen Purpose Driven as a method to infuse
church growth in a plateaued church. However, Purpose Driven
is not a church growth program. As a matter of fact, Rick warns
church leaders at every conference NOT to take these principles
home to their churches and implement them totally and
quickly. The change is too radical, too fast, and will have
disastrous repercussions for the church—particularly for the
church leader who attempts to introduce them. Rick says,
"There will most likely be bloodshed . . . and it will be yours!"

Dan Southerland has written the textbook for changing a
church from program driven to purpose driven. In his book,
Transitioning, Dan outlines the methodical process for change
in a church. While Dan addresses purpose driven transitions,
my task and calling is in training church planters to start new
purpose driven churches. There are several, easily noticeable
distinctives of new purpose driven churches.

Purpose Driven Churches are Culturally Relevant

The challenge is the same for every generation of pastors
and church leaders. How do we communicate what is timeless
and unchanging to a society that is rapidly changing? When
I contemplate the speed of technological advancements in
my generation alone, I can almost feel the winds of change
blowing past me. While black and white television finds its
way into the Smithsonian as a historic relic, a new level of
television utopia has exploded on the scene—high-definition
television (HDTV).

Purpose driven churches are the HDTVs of today; a church
with improved clarity and higher resolve to do whatever it

takes to present Christ to this generation. In the middle of a rapidly changing culture we need a church that speaks the language of this generation, not the language of our grandfather's generation. We need churches that will use today's technology to present the transforming message of Christ with impeccable clarity. We need a place where people risk new methodology to reach a culture we have never reached before.

Purpose driven churches are bringing striking clarity to the mission of the church in this century. They are focused with a laser-like intensity on reaching a segment of our population virtually untouched by the traditional church—the unchurched. Aubrey Malphurs writes in *Advanced Strategic Planning,* "I noted that in 1988 between 80 to 85% of churches in North America had either plateaued or were in decline

> *The vast majority of churches today are in need of intensive care, and many are on life support because we have lost sight of the mission of our Savior . . .*

(dying). As we enter the twenty-first century, that figure has not changed appreciably despite a valiant surge in church planting."[4] The vast majority of churches today are in need of intensive care, and many are on life support because we have lost sight of the mission of our Savior: *"For the Son of Man came to seek and to save what was lost."* (Luke 19:10 NIV)

Purpose Driven Churches Attract Larger Crowds

With a focus on reaching the unchurched, many purpose driven churches attract large crowds. Rick Warren writes, "You grow a church from the outside in, not the inside out. This is opposite the advice given by most books on church planting." This one distinctive is the hardest to flesh out in the church. We have been taught for decades that you grow a church from the inside out, not the outside in. We have been taught to start with a core of believers, and disciple them to reach your community. This process sounds solid, and almost biblical. However, the New Testament Church did not start that way in Acts 2. The New Testament Church launched large not small.

> *Those who accepted his message were baptized, and*
> *about three thousand were added to their number*
> *that day.* (Acts 2:41 NIV)

Two of our recent church starts have attracted large crowds. Church at the Bay, a new purpose driven church in Tampa, Florida launched large in 2005. In their first two months they averaged over 250 people in attendance each weekend. My brother-in-law, Phil Wilson, launched The Bridge Fellowship in Nashville, Tennessee in 2005 averaging over 260 in the first two months. Both of these churches grew to more than twice the size of the average church in America in only two months. We train purpose driven church planters to launch large from the very beginning of a new church. In Chapter 10 we will look into the methods necessary for launching large.

Purpose Driven Churches Embrace Change

We need a catalyst for reaching a new generation, but that catalyst is often difficult to find in existing non-purpose driven churches. We have unknowingly hidden the timeless relevance of Scripture behind traditional trimmings that are irrelevant to this generation. We have made the methods as sacred as the message. Most pastors have been taught to preserve the past rather than to embrace the future. Church @ The Springs began in 1994 as a purpose driven church seeking to be relevant to this generation. We have learned that relevance is a moving target that takes hard work and always involves change. Even though we are a relatively young church, we learned recently we have to keep challenging our methodology.

In 2003, we realized that Church @ The Springs was getting older. The median age had crept up to forty-two-years old. We had always focused on young families with children. In January of 2004 we strategically gave The Springs a facelift. We invested in computerized lighting and video upgrades. We intentionally changed the age of our music, adding more performance music and more visual enhancement with streaming video. We tightened up the service flow and length. In nine months, The Springs' median age dropped to thirty-four-years old while increasing in attendance by 200 people. During this same time period, we saw over 100 people commit their lives to Christ. Our Purpose Driven DNA remained the same, but our presentation changed to match our target.

One Christian man who is a member of an established church in our city invites unbelievers to The Springs. When asked why he doesn't invite them to his church he replied, "They wouldn't understand my church." He comes from a great church that teaches truth. However, to the eyes of this unchurched generation, the truth is hidden behind stained glass, eighteenth-century pews, and the music of bygone generations. While our heritage is great, lost people are not interested in our heritage. They want to know *who* God is and if he is relevant to their lives *today.*

Purpose Driven Churches are Christ-Called

Even if a church utilizes the technology and terminology of this generation, it will be lost without the proper power source. There are many churches springing up around the country with good technology, financial resources, and strategies; but they are having very little impact on this generation. Dozens of church starters have told me the glamour of a bold new work dulled for them long ago. Their dreams were dashed by the reality of the church-starting graveyard. I have heard pastors lament, "I know God called me, but why won't anyone show up for a service?"

Many church starters wind up feeling discarded in a pile of broken dreams. They are financially depleted, emotionally exhausted, and wondering what went wrong. Unfortunately, it is not enough to simply *want* to start a new church. The best human resources available cannot take the place of our Divine resource. Jesus Christ is still the one who builds the church. Jesus reminds us in John 15:5b (NIV), *". . . apart from me you can do nothing."*

The power to press on in the challenging days of church starting is the same power source who calls you in the first place. Remember, the calling to start a new church is not a career choice—it is God's invitation to join him. The Springs was birthed out of my personal walk with God and his subsequent call on my life. With that in mind, this book is about what he has taught me and allowed me to experience through The Springs, principles that are transferable to the lives of other church starters. It is also about the lessons I have learned from other leaders—lessons of leadership in starting and leading a purpose driven church, all grounded in a calling from God to join him.

One last thought about HDTVs: the price will keep most people from running out and purchasing one today. The same is true of starting a purpose driven church. The price tag is extremely high. This journey is not for the faint-hearted; there will be potholes, detours, and enemy attacks. A purpose driven church is an expensive model—and I am not talking just about finances. There are countless hours of preparation and planning, and long months spent recruiting and training your launch team. The first year is an exhausting roller coaster of emotions. The highest thrills and the lowest frustrations will frequent the early days of a church start. However, if you pay the price, and turn it on, it will be brighter, clearer, and more compelling than most churches you have seen. Feel the wonder of seeing it power up in living color, as unchurched people encounter a New Testament Church for this generation. Watch lives light up as they experience more of God's power than they have ever imagined.

The stories of purpose driven churches are being written even now through the experiences and journeys of countless thousands around the world. Join the ranks of those starting purpose driven churches. Come and explore the very edge of possibility, and I am confident you will see what you have never seen before. You heart will beat faster than it ever has. Then, contribute your own chapters of faith. Starting a purpose driven church can be the greatest adventure of your lifetime. Don't miss it!

---

[1] Warren, Rick, *The Purpose Driven Church: Growth Without Compromising Your Message & Mission*, (Grand Rapids, Mich.: Zondervan, 1995), 104–108.

[2] Malphurs, Aubrey, *Advanced Strategic Planning: A New Model for Church and Ministry Leaders*, (Grand Rapids, Mich.: Baker Books, 1999), 1.

[3] Warren, *The Purpose Driven Church*, 104–108.

[4] Malphurs, *Advanced Strategic Planning*, 2.

CHAPTER 2

Do We *Really* Need More Churches?

Since you are reading this book, you probably realize the importance of starting new churches, and you may even be thinking of starting one yourself. It may surprise you to read this, but not everyone believes starting new churches is a good idea. I talk regularly with church starters who are dealing with criticism from local pastors. I hope this chapter will strengthen your resolve when critics cross your path.

First of all, the territorial mindset of some pastors amazes me. They give many reasons to keep new churches out of their area. Some of the most prevalent arguments are:

(1) Since we cannot fill existing churches, we do not need new ones.

(2) Starting a new church will cause division in existing churches.

(3) Our church is not large enough to give up people to start a new church.

However, the more I study the need to reach our country for Christ, the more passionate I become about church starting. Following are some compelling reasons to continue starting churches everywhere in the United States.

Spiritually, We Are Losing America

Dave Olson, Director of Church Planting for the Evangelical Covenant Church, has researched ten years of consecutive attendance data from 300,000 Christian churches in America.

According to Olson, 3,200 churches close their doors each year in America, while 3,600 new churches, that ultimately survive, are started each year. This results in a net gain of 4,600 churches from 1990–2000. However, in order to have kept up with the current population growth during that same time period, we would have needed a net gain of 38,802 new churches.[1] In fact,

> – – – ➡
>
> *If the current trend for church attendance continues in America, by 2050 only 11.7% of America will attend church.*
>
> ⬅ – – –

in the last decade, the combined membership of all Protestant denominations has declined by 9.5%, while the national population has increased by 11.4%.[2] Of the fifty states, only Hawaii saw an increase in percentage of population attending church any given weekend from 1990–2000.[3] According to The North American Mission Board:

> In 1900, there were 27 churches for every 10,000 Americans.
> In 1950, there were 17 churches for every 10,000 Americans.
> In 2000, there were 12 churches for every 10,000 Americans.
> In 2004, there were 11 churches for every 10,000 Americans.[4]

If the current trend for church attendance continues in America, by 2050 only 11.7% of America will attend church.[5] The Barna Group reports that the number of unchurched adults has nearly doubled from 1991 to 2004. A Barna study explained, "Since 1991, the adult population in the United States has grown by 15%. During that same period, the number of adults who do not attend church has nearly doubled, rising from 39 million to 75 million—a 92% increase!"[6]

Clearly, we are losing ground with each passing year. We have a growing evangelistic deficit in America that will best be answered by starting new churches.

New Churches Are More Effective in Reaching Lost People

C. Peter Wagner, author of *Church Planting for a Greater Harvest*, says, "The single most effective evangelistic methodology under heaven is planting new churches."[7] Dave Olson says, "The strength of Christianity in the United States is based on over 300 years of starting new churches. Church planting is the most powerful growth mechanism for the American Church."[8]

After a church is three-years old it is half as effective in reaching people for Christ as it was in the early years of its existence. Once a church is fifteen-years old, it becomes one third as effective.[9]

The simple truth is, new churches reach more new people, and established churches reach more established people. For example, The Springs is less effective at reaching the lost today than when we first began. Initially over 75% of our people found Christ at The Springs. Today that number is closer to 60%.

Statistically the larger and older a church is, the less likely it is to successfully evangelize. It is like trying to fight the aging process. We can do all we can to look better on the outside, but eventually we have to face the truth—we're getting older! The best way to fight the evangelistic decline is to start new churches. Ralph Moore writes in his book, *Starting a New Church*, "One American denomination recently found that 80% of its converts came to Christ in churches less than 2 years old."[10]

New Churches Grow Faster than Established Churches

Sadly, 80% to 85% of American churches are on the downside of their life cycle. Aubrey Malphurs writes in *Planting Growing Churches for the 21st Century*, "Of the 15% that are growing, 14% are growing as the result of transfer rather than conversion growth."[11] Since 1965, most mainline denominations have been in decline. According to Bill Easum, author of *Beyond the Box: Innovative Churches That Work*, "Studies show that if a denomination wishes to reach more people, the number of new churches it begins each year must equal at least 3% of the denomination's existing churches. Based on this formula, mainline denominations are failing to plant enough churches to offset their decline."[12]

In the average year, half of all churches do not add one new member through conversion growth. Most of their growth is people coming from other churches. Jesus said we are to be fishers of men, not swappers of fish from aquarium to aquarium! Conversely, healthy new churches often experience exponential growth.

New churches think externally. They are more focused on reaching new people because evangelism is their primary purpose. By contrast, established churches fight the centrifugal pull of thinking externally and caring for their members. The older and larger a church becomes, the more time and resources the leaders must give to their members. The resources spent in the early days of a church reaching new people are now spent caring for existing members. Good or bad, this fact is one of the contributing factors to slowing the evangelistic zeal in an established church.

People Are More Open to Change in New Churches

New congregations carry less institutional baggage, meaning they are more likely to respond to a changing culture than established churches. The Springs, for instance, moved fourteen times in our first eight years, and our church was excited about each move. Implanted in our church from its inception was a mindset that change would be a constant. New churches attract and are led by pioneers. Pioneers go where no one has gone before and take risks. Established churches normally attract settlers more than pioneers. For pioneering spirits, change is a horse they ride until they can break it and subdue it. Once changes are made, they search for the next wild stallion to break. Change is built into the DNA of most new churches. The phrase "we've never done it that way before" is irrelevant. Everything is new!

Change always brings a level of discomfort or pain, much like lifting weights initially brings pain to the muscles you just worked out. After the pain subsides, growth and development in the muscles takes place. Healthy change brings growth in our lives and churches. Remember, change, pain, and then growth.

> ----➔
> *Change is built into the DNA of most new churches. The phrase "we've never done it that way before" is irrelevant. Everything is new!*
> ◄----

Many rebel against the change and start screaming at the pain stage. Unfortunately those people miss the growth part of the cycle altogether.

Ralph Moore writes in *Starting a New Church*, "Decisions emerge quickly in new congregations; the process moves more and more slowly as a church grows older."[13] The Springs is a living example of this truth. We used to be able to implement changes rapidly. However, the larger a church becomes, the slower the change process. If you change an established church too quickly, it is similar to taking a sharp turn with a 2,000 passenger cruise liner. Inevitably, someone is going to throw up on you.

New churches also speak the language of the next generation. A recent trend is for established churches to begin new contemporary services to reach the next generation. An endeavor to be commended, but we often fall short when an aging pastor attempts to communicate to a younger audience. New churches are often led by younger pastors who know the subtleties of the culture. What they lack in experience, they make up for with pioneering spirits that effectively reach a new generation. We need to build alliances between seasoned veterans and our young church leaders. We need to partner experience with youth to reach the next generation.

For this reason, Purpose Driven Planting is beginning Coaching Networks around the country, connecting seasoned veterans of church starts with new church starters. The goal is to decrease the failure rate of new church starts. To learn about the latest coaching opportunities through Purpose Driven Planting, go to *www.pdplanting.com*.

Starting new churches is the hope for turning America around again. There is a resurgence of interest in church planting in this generation. Ed Stetzer reports that between 1980 and 2000, over 50,000 churches were planted in North America.[14] However, even with that good news, the church planting rate today is only half what it was in the 1950s.[15] We need to help church planters grow healthy vibrant churches, changing and reshaping their generation for Christ.

---

[1] Olson, David T., "Quick Facts on the American Church," *The American Church*, <u>Top Ten Most Popular Downloads</u>, 2006, **www.theamericanchurch.org**, *http://theamericanchurch.org/sample/ QuickFacts.ppt#342,13,Slide13*

[2] Clegg, Tom , *How to Plant a Church in the 21ˢᵗ Century*, Seminar, 1997.

[3] Olson, David T., "12 Surprising Facts about the American Church," *The State of the Church*, <u>The Nation</u>, 2004. **www.theamericanchurch.org**, *http://theamericanchurch.org/ sample/12SurprisingFactsSample.ppt#320,9,Slide9*

[4] Stetzer, Edward J., An Analysis of the Church Planting Process and Other Selected Factors on the Attendence of SBC Church Plants. A NAMB Self Study. May 2003, *http://www.churchplantingvillage .net/atf/cf%7B087EF6B4-D6ES-4BBF-BED1-7893D360F394%7D/ Summary_of_the_Study.pdf*

[5] Olson, "Quick Facts on the American Church," *http:// theamericanchurch.org/sample/QuickFacts.ppt#337,8,Slide8*

[6] Barna Group, The, *The Barna Update*, **www.barna.org**, *http://www.barna.org/FlexPage.aspx?Page=BarnaUpdate&BarnaUpdateID= 163*, May 4, 2004.

[7] Wagner, C. Peter, *Church Planting for a Greater Harvest: A Comprehensive Guide* (Ventura, Calif.: Regal Books, 1991), 11.

[8] Olson, Dave, *The State of the Church*, www.theamericanchurch.org, 2004.

[9] Malphurs, Aubrey, *Planting Growing Churches for the 21st Century: A Comprehensive Guide for New Churches and Those Desiring Renewal.* (Grand Rapids, Mich.: Baker Books, 2004) 44.

[10] Moore, Ralph, *Starting a New Church: The Church Planter's Guide to Success.* (Ventura, Calif.: Regal Books, 2002), 23.

[11] Malphurs, *Planting Growing Churches*, 32.

[12] Easum, Bill, "Church Planting," *Welcome to Easum, Bandy, and Associates*, 2003–2006, **www.easumbandy.com**, *http://www .easumbandy.com/resources/index.php?action=details&records=1062*

[13] Moore, *Starting a New Church*, 25.

[14] Stetzer, Ed, *Planting New Churches in a Postmodern Age.* (Nashville, Tenn.: Broadman & Holman, 2003), 11.

[15] Olson, "Quick Facts on the American Church," *http://theamericanchurch.org/sample/QuickFacts.ppt#344,15,Slide15*

CHAPTER 3

Why Start a Purpose Driven Church?

We live in the age of multiple choices. Every day of our lives we are inundated with choices about everything, from what we drink to what we drive. The same myriad of options are available to anyone starting a new church today. From cell churches to post-modern churches to traditional churches to house churches, our options are endless. We even have options within the models, from leadership structure to worship style.

The many church planting models available to church planters today can present a daunting decision amid all the choices. The downside of so many options is the temptation to use the "smorgasbord approach" when church planting—that is, combining several models. The results are typically unfavorable, as the many models sometimes contradict one another, leaving the church planter dissatisfied and hungry for a healthy new church. For that reason, find a model that resonates with you, study and pray through it, then commit to it and stand by your choice. You can adapt the model once you have a growing healthy church, but in order to get off the launch pad without a misfire, follow the model.

When Teddi and I attended the *Purpose Driven Church Conference* in 1995, there were about 120 people attending The Springs and our church had no clear strategy to fulfill our purpose. At the conference, we were overwhelmed with what we heard. It was like trying to drink from a fire hydrant. But Rick Warren has a unique gift for making complex issues simple to understand; and with each successive session, our church strategy crystallized. "Purpose Driven" was the model and process to drive the calling God put on our lives. Teddi and I were so excited! It felt like we had just been handed all the answers for an upcoming comprehensive final exam.

However, Rick warned us at the conference not to change our churches as soon as we came home. But to a young pastor, that was like telling a five-year-old they could not open their Christmas presents until December 26th. We came home from the PDC Conference and implemented everything we learned. By implementing the Purpose Driven DNA too quickly in our young church, we lost our entire leadership team. The vision was too vast a departure from what they believed The Springs should look like. If I had known about the Purpose Driven DNA before we started The Springs, we could have started correctly and saved ourselves a lot of pain and heartache. (Fortunately, this story has a happy ending. Within three months after the loss of our leadership team, The Springs began to see steady growth that has not stopped in over ten years.)

In a study of over 600 church plants from 2000–2002, Ed Stetzer reports that church planters who used the Purpose Driven Model saw the greatest impact on mean attendance, over the other models. The diagram on page 29 is from the study showing the first four years of mean attendance by comparison with those churches that did not use the Purpose Driven Model.[1]

The statistics support Purpose Driven as the fastest growing model in church planting; but increasing numbers

Purpose Driven Churches

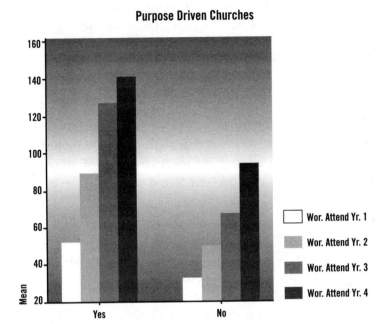

are not the only reason for starting a purpose driven church. In order to assist the church planter in making an educated decision, this chapter will explore the distinctives of a Purpose Driven Church.

The Purpose Driven Church is a Biblical Model

The Purpose Driven Church is built around five biblical purposes. Dan Morgan, Director of the Nehemiah Project for Church Planting, writes "God's purposes for His church should be the dominant consideration in decisions about *what the church does and how it organizes itself.*[2] A study of the Bible led Rick [Warren] to summarize God's purposes for the church into five overarching purposes anchored in two passages of Scripture. The Scripture passages are the Great Commandment and the Great Commission."

> Purpose Driven is not about seeker services. It is
> about evangelism. Purpose Driven is a process by
> which you bring people in through evangelism, raise
> them up through discipleship, train them for
> ministry, and send them out on mission to the glory
> of God.
>
> — Rick Warren, 04/05/2001

We do not create the purpose for the church; however, every generation of church leaders must rediscover God's purposes. The purposes of the church are found in the beginning of the New Testament Church in Jerusalem:

> *They devoted themselves to the apostles' teaching
> and to the fellowship, to the breaking of bread and
> to prayer. Everyone was filled with awe, and many
> wonders and miraculous signs were done by the
> apostles. All the believers were together and had
> everything in common. Selling their possessions and
> goods, they gave to anyone as he had need. Every
> day they continued to meet together in the temple
> courts. They broke bread in their homes and ate
> together with glad and sincere hearts, praising God
> and enjoying the favor of all the people. And the
> Lord added to their number daily those who were
> being saved.* (Acts 2:42–47 NIV)

As a new church grows, it must balance the five purposes to become healthy.

In the first church we observe them teaching each other (Discipleship), enjoying fellowship together (Fellowship), worshiping together (Worship), and ministering to the needs of people (Ministry) while people were being saved daily (Evangelism).

As a new church grows, it must balance the five purposes to become healthy. The tendency for every pastor is to build the church on his own passions and strengths. Without intending to neglect God's other purposes for the church, we can build an out-of-balance church. Some churches are heavy in teaching and light on ministry. Some are strong in worship and weak in evangelism. Others are focused on ministering to the community and fuzzy on fellowship. All five purposes must be balanced and re-balanced in the growth of a purpose driven church in order to follow the example of the New Testament church.

The Purpose Driven Church Advocates "Crowd to Core Growth"

This "Crowd to Core Growth" distinctive makes Purpose Driven a more effective approach for church planting. Most other models follow a core to crowd approach when starting a church. They begin, for example, with a small group of people meeting for Bible studies, and slowly grow the church from the inside out to reach the community. However, purpose driven churches are not planted from a core, they are launched from a crowd.

Rick Warren teaches that it is easier to build a church from a crowd than it is to build a crowd from a church. For this reason, the weekend service is designed to draw a crowd of people and create an air of excitement. One of the most common complaints about church is that it is boring or irrelevant. The church of the living Christ should be anything but boring and irrelevant. We should be capturing people's attention with the amazing truth of God's love for them, realizing that whatever gets your attention eventually gets you. We want people to walk out of the services saying, "I can't wait for next week." Once we capture their attention, we can capture their hearts. The concentric circles below demonstrate the crowd to core process of a purpose driven church.

Start by reaching the community on the outer circle, and move them toward the core in the inner circle. Focus on the community and attract a crowd, turn the crowd into a congregation, the congregation into committed Christ followers, and the committed into the core. The ultimate goal is to move people into deeper levels of commitment, then send them back out to reach the community for Christ.

The Purpose Driven Church Focuses on Reaching the Lost

Jesus did not want his followers to lose sight of their purpose after he ascended. In Matthew 28:19–20 (NIV), he gave them the Great Commission, *"Therefore go and make disciples of all nations, baptizing them in the name of the Father and of the Son and of the Holy Spirit, and teaching them to obey everything I have commanded you. And surely I am with you always, to the very end of the age."*

In line with Jesus' teaching, purpose driven churches target hell-bound people. Rick Warren says, "The church that forgets the ultimate is driven by the immediate." The ultimate for purpose driven churches is targeting people who are far from God. The already-convinced Christian is not our target, but is welcome to join us as we reach the lost. We want to make it hard to go to hell from Ocala. Our people know and understand that it takes unselfish people to reach the lost. Rick Warren says it best in the first line of *The Purpose Driven Life*, "It's not about you."[3]

The concept of targeting in regard to churches turned me off when I first heard it; therefore, I fully understand voices in postmodern church life raising concerns about it. Targeting does tend to sound more like a marketing ploy rather than a church principle. My initial defenses went up immediately. I thought, *God wants all people to come to know him, not just a targeted segment of the population.*

> - - - ➤
> *"Targeting is actually a process of determining who the planter can best reach first and most effectively, but welcoming all seekers and expecting target groups to multiply as the church grows."*
> ◄ - - -

Dan Morgan says, "The most common misconception about targeting is that it is a process of excluding people the planter doesn't want to reach. Targeting is actually a process of determining who the planter can best reach first and most effectively, but welcoming all seekers and expecting target groups to multiply as the church grows."[4] Obviously, no church reaches everybody, which is why there is plenty of room for many different styles of churches, because God created all kinds of people. Effective churches focus on who they want to reach. In every church, there is a bulls-eye target, whether we want to admit it or not. The bulls-eye is who you can most effectively reach first. Certainly every target has larger outer rings around the bulls-eye, and as the church grows, so does the diversity of the congregation.

Once the target within a church is defined, build a worship experience to reach that target. In the first few months of The Springs, we simply created worship experiences that I liked. The result was that we reached people like me: Christians who were looking for a casual environment and more contemporary forms of worship. Our first flood of seventy-five people came from other churches in the area. Once we defined our target as the unchurched, it changed the way I communicated, the music we sang, and the flow of the worship experience. Since targeting brings incredible clarity, once we began designing worship experiences to reach the unchurched, we began to attract the unchurched.

The Purpose Driven Church Has a Simple Structure

Ultimately, streamlining church bureaucracy makes a church more effective for the kingdom. Rick Warren has said that in the church "we have taken an American form of government and married it with the Bride of Christ. The result is a church that is as effective as the government!"[5] We have complicated the church with so many layers of bureaucracy that it renders the church ineffective. Purpose driven churches lend themselves to simplifying the structures, resulting in clarifying the focus of your church.

Dan Morgan says, "Time spent in committees and in business meetings is time people can't invest in ministry to others. A purpose-driven church is staff led with congregational input, especially in areas that directly affect members' time and money."

Make the complex simple; that's what Jesus did. An organization with a complex structure is difficult to duplicate in a new church. Streamline structures to minimize time spent in meetings and maximize time spent changing lives. Purpose driven churches cut people loose to get in the trenches and to be a part of life change.

The Purpose Driven Church Has a Simple Path to Maturity

The result of targeting the unchurched, combined with focusing on attracting a weekend crowd, is rapid growth by evangelism. With rapid growth, a purpose driven church needs to quickly assimilate many new believers. Rick Warren says, "Instead of trying to grow a *church* with *programs*, focus on growing *people* with a *process*."[6]

Purpose driven churches use a method that follows a simple path to maturity, from seeker to reproducing disciple. The Baseball Diamond below is a visual of the spiritual growth process in a purpose driven church:

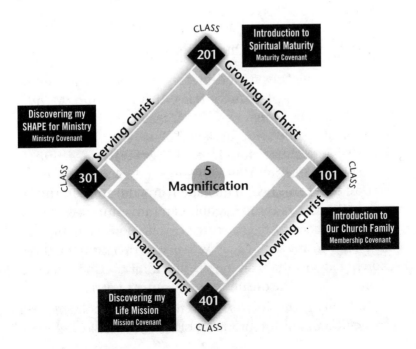

At each base, representing a "next step" toward God, a class is taught on that particular purpose in the life of a Christ-follower. The goal is to move people on to deeper levels of commitment, as they assimilate themselves into the life of the church. The simplicity and reproducibility of the Purpose Driven CLASS system makes it simple for a church start to implement. People are encouraged to move systematically through the classes. First base is CLASS 101: Discovering Membership. Second base is CLASS 201: Discovering Spiritual Maturity. Third base is CLASS 301: Discovering Your Ministry. And home plate is CLASS 401: Discovering Your Life Mission.

Once a member has attended all of the classes, they know the foundational purposes for their existence as a Christ-follower. As they learn each purpose in depth, they weave their life deeper into the fabric of the local church, and become closer to God. The classes are not for information, but for the transformation of their lives within the church. Each class is designed to move the Christ-follower toward a deeper commitment to Christ.

The Purpose Driven Church is Reproducible

The Purpose Driven Model represents a paradigm shift for many in church planting circles. It is not simply a new methodology, but a renewed way of seeing the church in the twenty-first century. Not just a new church, but a rediscovery of a New Testament church for this generation of church planters. Dan Morgan writes, "The methods of Saddleback can be copied, and the closer the setting is to Saddleback, the better they will work. But when adopted as a way of viewing the church, it becomes a flexible and adaptable framework to guide any planter in any setting in how to develop a healthy, balanced church that will attain all the size and ministry God intended when he placed the dream in that planter's heart."[7]

Not only is the Purpose Driven Model reproducible and cross-cultural, but it reproduces other churches as well. The

Springs has started ten other churches locally and nationally, and Saddleback started twenty-five churches in their first fifteen years. Simply put, a healthy purpose driven church starts other healthy purpose driven churches.

Purpose Driven Church Planters "Learn and Return"

Our family has great memories of Disney World in Orlando. During the Christmas season of 2003, we went to Mickey's Very Merry Christmas Party. As we walked down Main Street, manufactured snow was falling from the sky, Christmas music was playing, and the park was filled with people. The main event of the evening

Purpose driven churches lend their shoulders to little brothers unable to see the parade. They allow you to climb up and examine the view from their perspective.

was the Christmas Parade. By the time we arrived, people were standing three and four deep to view the parade. The only way Luke, our youngest son, was going to see the parade was to climb up on my shoulders. Luke was a big boy for his age, weighing in at that time at almost seventy pounds. This old man's shoulders and back got tired quickly. I soon passed him off to his big brothers, Jared and Jacob. We shared the load during the parade. Luke loved it and could not stop talking about it. Without our shoulders, he would have missed the parade.

Purpose driven churches lend their shoulders to little brothers unable to see the parade. They allow you to climb up and examine the view from their perspective. The parade does not consist of make-believe characters, but real life people. We get to see and be part of a parade of freshly redeemed lives. At the heart of the Purpose Driven Church movement is what I call the "learn and return" factor. Purpose driven churches allow others to glean from what they have learned, freely returning wisdom to the Kingdom. Purpose driven churches lock arms with those coming up behind them in the journey. Today there are over 700 megachurches in the United States, while there were only ten of them thirty years ago.[8] I believe the explosion of church growth is largely due to this one principle of "learn and return."

Fading away is the territorial nature that has hampered the growth and unity of the church universal. A new breed of church leader is emerging, eager to share what they have learned. Jim Cymbala in his book, *The Life God Blesses*, writes, "A humble heart is like a magnet that draws the favor of God toward us."[9] I have watched the truth of this statement in the lives of church leaders God is using around the world. They generously share the knowledge the Holy Spirit has revealed to them with other pastors and church leaders.

As Paul admonished Timothy in 2 Timothy 2:2 (MSG) *Pass on what you heard from me . . . to reliable leaders who are competent to teach others.* Keep looking over your shoulder, because someone is following. Someone is three steps behind you, who needs to discover what you have already learned. Reach back, grab their hand, and allow them to climb on your shoulders. The parade of freshly redeemed lives is about to begin.

Purpose driven churches are biblical, crowd to core, focused on reaching the lost, have simple structures, follow a simple path to maturity, and are reproducible no matter what city or culture you are called to reach for Christ. Purpose Driven is the most effective strategy for the twenty-first century church.

---

[1] Stetzer, Ed, *An Analysis of the Church Planting Process*, **www.newchurches.com**, 2003, 7.

[2] Morgan, Dan, *Overview of Purpose Driven Church Planting*, paper presented at Purpose Driven Church Conference. (Lake Forest, Calif.: Saddleback Church), 2005.

[3] Warren, Rick, *The Purpose Driven Life: What on Earth Am I Here For?* (Grand Rapids, Mich.: Zondervan, 2002), 17.

[4] Morgan, *Overview of Purpose Driven Church Planting*.

[5] Warren, Rick, *Breaking the 200–300 Barrier*, seminar.

[6] Warren, Rick, *The Purpose Driven Church*, (Grand Rapids, Mich.: Zondervan), 1995, 110.

[7] Morgan, *Overview of Purpose Driven Church Planting*.

[8] Ibid.

[9] Cymbala, Jim, *Fresh Faith*, (Grand Rapids, Mich.: Zondervan, 1999), 87.

CHAPTER 4

Should *You* Start a Church?

Think about all the energy and financial resources that go into a church start, and then realize that the majority of new churches fail in the first year. How can something that starts out looking so good, fail? Many times throughout the years, I have sat down with a church starter and listened while he described the unraveling of his dream, coupled with the evaporation of his personal finances and a struggling marriage. Nothing dies harder than a dream to which we have given our lives. If God is really interested in advancing his kingdom, why do so many of his churches fail? God never fails, we do.

As I said in Chapter 1, I've watched many church planters with all the right ingredients—the right strategy, good financial resources, good teachers, right demographics—fail. They followed all the conference notes from the professionals, and they failed. They had everything but the main thing, a calling from God, which is the first and most

> *Nothing dies harder than a dream to which we have given our lives.*

important ingredient for the foundation of a successful church start. You must start by confirming God's calling on your life.

Confirm God's Calling

Has God really called you to start a church? The truth is, many church starters talk themselves into starting a church. Some are disgruntled staff members who think they can lead better than their senior pastor. Others see the church dying and think a new style of worship is the answer.

> ----→
> *Starting a church is about a personal calling and your journey with God. Do not just duplicate a new church-starting methodology, follow your calling.*
> ←- - -

Others have watched new churches around the country explode with growth, and think, *I can do that!* The first question I ask a church starter is, "Has God called you to start a church?" Is this God's idea or your idea? Has God confirmed this new endeavor for your life or have you been lured at the latest conference? Is this a *good* idea or a *God* idea? Because good ideas never build strong churches; "God ideas" build strong churches. Don't underestimate the power of your calling.

Starting a church is about a *personal* calling and your journey with God. Do not just duplicate a new church-starting methodology, follow *your* calling.

"Calling" is a fuzzy word that has been watered down, and mystified in the ministry. How can you define it to someone? A calling is personal; it's the voice of God in your life. Henry Blackaby writes in *Experiencing God*, "If you have trouble hearing God speak, you are in trouble at the very heart of your Christian experience."[1] A calling comes from a relationship—not with vocational training, nor simply a career path. Many church starters fail because they have misunderstood God's calling for their life. God loves them, and may have called them to ministry, but not to start a church.

Starting a church and pastoring an established church require very different gifts and abilities. Just as there are specialized positions for professional athletes on a team, an established pastor and a church starter are specialized positions in ministry. A church starter has a different skill set and calling than an established pastor. A church starter is a risk taker and an entrepreneur. He must be a generalist and wear many hats to get a church off the ground. Most pastors of established churches are specialists who function well in a structure. In new churches there is no structure, it must be created. Change is the only constant in a new church and a church starter must be able to make decisions quickly.

If you are wrestling with starting a church, first and foremost, get alone with God. Shut out the noise and distractions around you, and take a personal retreat to confirm God's calling on your life. After God called us to begin The Springs, I went to a cabin in the mountains where I locked myself away for nearly a week. It was me, my Bible, and the Father. I was scared to death about the future, and I needed to hear my Father's voice and get his direction. I turned to Psalm 37, the Scripture God had given me to confirm my calling:

> *Trust in the Lord and do good;*
> *dwell in the land and enjoy safe pasture.*
> *Delight yourself in the Lord and he will give you*
> *the desires of your heart.*
> *Commit your way to the Lord;*
> *trust in him and he will do this:*
> *He will make your righteousness shine like the dawn,*
> *the justice of your cause like the noonday sun.*
> (Psalm 37:3–6 NIV)

I was to begin a church in Ocala, Florida with no money and no formal training. What I did have was a calling from my heavenly Father.

In the process of determining your calling, make the investment and get an assessment. Many denominations offer and even require church planter assessments prior to supporting a church planter. This investment of time and finances will be invaluable to your journey. If you are not connected with an association or denomination, you can go to Ed Stetzer's church planting Web site, *www.NewChurches.com* and find the information. Ed offers a wide variety of free resources and experience. Avail yourself of them. You may also search the Internet for "Church Planter Assessment" to locate new assessments.

In addition, church starters are called to specific locations, to a certain place. God prepares a place for you and you for a place. Rick Warren talks about God calling him to Orange County, California to begin Saddleback Church. Ed Young talks about God calling him to Dallas, Texas to begin Fellowship Church. Honestly, I begged God to allow me to leave Ocala. I had grown up in a large city, but Ocala is not a very large city. Presently it's a city of 50,000 people in a county of 300,000— a smaller population than any other place we had lived before.

When God called us to start a church, we really thought maybe we were going back home to Orlando. Maybe God would even lead us to Atlanta or Birmingham. I will never forget the day that God gave us the location. I was on the back porch having my quiet time when God impressed on my heart that we were going to start the church in Ocala. I remember walking off the back porch into the house, looking at Teddi and saying, "He's going to make us stay in Ocala."

Teddi looked at me and said, "Go back and ask him again!" She felt the same way I did about the *where* of our calling. We wanted to leave. Why wouldn't God let us leave?

Do you know why God wanted us to stay in Ocala? After living here for five years, I had learned the demographics and I fit in with the culture of the city. I had become an Ocalan. I was not from Ocala, but I knew Ocala. And God said, "This is home. You can reach these people. They are your people." God needed an Ocalan to reach Ocala.

Fit the Culture

I have met many church starters who want to reach upper class executives and their families. My first question is: Are you one of them? Whether we like it or not, we will reach those like us, not those *want* to reach. It's a law of

Whether we like it or not, we will reach those like us, not those we want to reach.

demographics. Studies show the number one reason people initially choose a church is because they identify with the pastor. Many church starters experience failure because they don't honestly know who they are, and target people who are not like them. It is an extremely rare person who is able to successfully minister to people who are vastly different socially and economically.

Whether we like it or not, there is a class system in the United States. We all fit somewhere. Reach who you are. Look at your relational world. Your closest friends can easily identify who you are best suited to reach with a new church. After you have identified those people, God will confirm the where of the church start.

One church starter insisted he was called to reach upper class people in a large city, even though his previous successful pastorates were in rural country locations in the Midwest. Years later, he is still trying to convince himself he can reach these people. His family is in financial ruin and he regularly questions his own faith in this journey. My heart breaks for him and his family. He is a gifted pastor serving in the wrong location. God has wired you to reach a specific group of people. So be honest about who you really are. And, if you can't get honest with yourself, then ask somebody else who you trust. Once you align your calling with a culture that fits you, you are on your way to stepping into an explosive church plant.

Are You Wired to Be a Church Starter?

Are you really wired to start a church? Since you are reading this book, you probably are at least considering a new church. Ralph Moore writes in *Starting a New Church*, "If you can live without this project, you

A church start has to be an all-consuming fire in your life.

probably should."[2] A church start has to be an all-consuming fire in your life. If you cannot get the thoughts of this new church out of your head, read on.

Are you a proven leader? Starting a church is all about strong leadership. If you do not have the gift of leadership, you are going to struggle. The leadership gift is the ability to cast vision, motivate, and direct people to harmoniously accomplish the purposes of God.

Vision casting is a huge piece of this leadership gift. If you cannot cast a vision big enough for people to get excited about, they will never follow you. Rick Warren recites an old Chinese proverb in the Purpose Driven Church Conference, "If you want to know if you are a leader, look over your shoulder. If no one is following you, you are simply taking a walk." With no leadership gifting, there are many church starters taking walks. But if you have the leadership gift, lead boldly! Romans 12:8 (NLT) says, *If God has given you leadership ability, take the responsibility seriously.*

A leader has the ability to engineer change in an organization. A new church will constantly be changing. Without constant change, it will die. Leaders know how to change to keep the church alive and growing, gaining momentum week by week.

Secondly, can you teach and capture people's attention? The gift of teaching is the ability to understand, clearly explain, and apply the word of God. This gift is evidenced by a widespread unsolicited affirmation of your preaching and teaching. Not the usual, "Nice sermon, Pastor!" If you do not have the gift of teaching, do not attempt to start a church. Many people in ministry believe they have both of these gifts. The sad truth is many pastors can't teach! They do not enjoy the process of message preparation, and their people do not enjoy the process of receiving their messages.

What do you have a heart for? What do you have a passion for? If you are going to start a church from scratch, you have to have a passion for the unchurched, for people that are far from God. Seeing someone bend their knee to Christ must energize your heart. There is nothing like watching a wayward person discover they matter so much to a God who loves them. You have to long to see the light go on in peoples' hearts.

There is nothing like watching a wayward person discover they matter so much to a God who loves them.

Jesus had a reputation—he was known as a friend of sinners. If we are going to begin churches we have to become friends of sinners. I was recently in an attorney's office for a mortgage closing. The attorney's assistant recognized me from the church because her children are members of The Springs. She introduced me to the attorney, and he asked what church I pastored. When I told him The Springs, he lit up and said, "I have been invited to that church so many times. But I'll tell you who is on me the hardest about coming to church there . . . my bartender! She said you have a great church."

That conversation might not seem complimentary; some pastors would not tell people that bartenders are inviting people to their church. But I wear that one like a badge of honor! We're penetrating the dark places. The name of our church is conversation in smoke-filled rooms flowing with liquor and foul language. We are friends of sinners. I love it!

Finally, if you are starting a new church, you must have a passion for the local church. You have to believe that the church is the hope of the world. That burning belief will just become larger in your heart, as it has mine at The Springs. There is nothing like the church when it's working right, when it's firing on all cylinders, when people are coming to Christ, growing in Christ, and living for Christ. And there is no greater calling than to bring a church into existence.

It is evaluation time. Can you confirm God's calling for you to plant a church? Do you fit the culture? Are you wired for starting a church? Ask yourself honestly if that is who you are. If it is not, read the next sentence very carefully. DO NOT DO THIS, GET OUT NOW, FIND SOMETHING ELSE TO DO WITH YOUR LIFE! Put this book down and run out of the room. God loves you, and has a plan for your life. Consider yourself warned about the dangers of starting a new church. And hopefully I have helped some avoid the heartache of a failed church start.

If after reading this chapter, you are convinced church starting is for you, you are in for the greatest adventure of your life. It is not for the faint-hearted. Church starters are the Navy Seals of the church. You must be highly-trained and disciplined. You are the Marines, the elite fighting force storming enemy territory. You must establish a beachhead where one does not exist, for this is an extreme ministry.

---

[1] Blackaby, Henry T. and Claude V. King, *Experiencing God: How to Live the Full Adventure of Knowing and Doing the Will of God.* (Nashville,Tenn.: Broadman & Holman, 1994), 36.

[2] Moore, Ralph, *Starting a New Church: The Church Planter's Guide to Success* (Ventura, Calif.: Regal Books, 2002), 35.

Dream Stage

- The Dream Stage
- Building a Launch Team
- Lessons from the Trenches

Dream	Design	Launch	Development	Strategic Leadership
0–3 Months	4–6 Months	6–8 Months	8–12 Months	1 Year and Beyond

Chapter 5

The Dream Stage

Have you ever taken a long distance trip in a car—with small children? Years ago, Teddi and I took our two young boys on a road trip from Jacksonville, Florida to Tennessee.

All the details of the trip had been taken care of. I even rigged up a television and game system in the back of the car. The road trip should have taken about ten hours. We headed north on I-95 looking for the exit to cut over to Atlanta. We had never traveled from Jacksonville before, but I was confident I could find the way without a map. We never found a sign for an exit to Atlanta off I-95, because there *were* no signs to Atlanta. At least I never saw any! Certainly we were going the wrong way, but I was excited to see signs for South of the Border, a restaurant reminiscent of some fun childhood memories of vacations with my parents. We stopped there to ask directions and ate lunch. The depressing news was given to us at lunch; we were six hours off course, and our ten-hour road trip became

Dream	Design	Launch	Development	Strategic Leadership
0–3 Months	4–6 Months	6–8 Months	8–12 Months	1 Year and Beyond

a sixteen-hour nightmare. A quick look at a map would have saved us six painful hours on the road.

For a church starter to begin this journey without a look at a map could prove to be disastrous. Mapping and preparing for the church starting experience is critical for the success of the church. Many of my greatest lessons have been learned by my mistakes, because pain is a tremendous instructor. Pain often leaves behind scarring that indelibly marks our memories. The Springs was painfully lacking in our strategy development, and indeed, *lacking* would be an understatement. We began with no map or training, and consequently fumbled through the first six months of our church. In fact, we did not get a look at a road map to our church's future until we attended our first Purpose Driven Church Conference. Finally, at six months old, we developed our strategy and the values that drive the church.

In essence, we lost six months of growth and maturity. Without core values, a strategy, and purposes in place, it cost us leadership, people, and momentum. But from the time we were six-months old until we were one-year old, we fast-

> "When you find the vision for your life, you won't take hold of it; it will take hold of you."

tracked the mapping process and made up for lost time. We were, in effect, playing catch up. Also important to note was that this time period was the only season of The Springs in which we experienced a plateau in attendance. We added new people, but lost the same number of people due to a lack of preparation.

Developing Our Vision

As it says in Proverbs 16:4 (NLT), *The Lord has made everything for his own purposes . . .* In fact, we are to be people of purpose— seeking out a cause to which we can give our lives. Bruce

Wilkinson says, "When you find the vision for your life, you won't take hold of it; it will take hold of you."[1] A vision is something that begins as a thought and eventually captures our hearts and lives. The reason you are reading this book is probably because a vision to start a new church is capturing your heart. You cannot ignore it anymore, because it is taking hold of you. The calling is getting clearer and clearer with each passing article you read or new church you see.

Vision is ever evolving in the heart of a purpose driven leader. You are in the process of vision development. Defining vision is like going for an eye exam. As you sit in the chair, the eye doctor places the different lenses over your eyes and asks you to read the letters on the wall. Changing the lenses and asking, "Which one looks clearer, one or two?" Then adjusting the lenses again, "Which one looks clearer now, one or two?" This is a frustrating exam for me, because as I go further into the test, one and two look similar. The decision is easy at first. One is so blurry and the other so clear. In the early days of a church start, you easily see the big vision for the church. It is the beginning of the "eye exam" for the church. The years ahead will continue to involve vision development, a clarifying and deepening of vision, and there will be years of further fine-tuning the growing vision of a maturing church. But now, we must begin with the initial requirement of a God-given vision.

Vision must first be God-given because the church was, and still is, his idea. When God wants a new church started and a city to be impacted by him, he taps someone on the shoulder and places a vision in their heart. Vision grows as God deepens and grows it in your consciousness. God clarified the vision for us and The Springs first through Church at Brook Hills in Birmingham, Alabama. This worship experience was our first, "is it number one or number two?" eye exam. When we walked in the lobby and heard the band kicking in the music for the service, it captured us. The people greeting us and giving us name tags exuded the warmth of the church. We felt at home, even though we had never been there and were over 500 miles from home. The vision was birthed in us.

As your God-given vision improves, it becomes more compelling in your life. I could not stop thinking about a new church. I was being consumed with the future of a church that had not yet begun. James Kouzes writes in Leadership Challenge, "A vision is a point on the horizon that will be reached only at some date in the future, a statement of what will be created years or decades ahead. To create visions, leaders must become preoccupied with the future."[2] In this visionary stage, an all-consuming search for the results of the fulfilled visions of other previously-started churches begins. Churches like Brook Hills, Saddleback, Willow Creek, Fellowship Church in Dallas, and North Point Community Church in Atlanta, were some fulfilled visions that clarified my vision.

Before telling someone about a vision for a new church, passion is required. When I meet with church starters who talk about their vision for a new work, generally after one meeting I can tell if the church will get off the ground or not. If they cannot convey their enthusiasm and get me excited about their vision for a new church, chances are they will struggle with casting the vision for a group of people. Nothing ignites and excites my heart more than talking about birthing a new church. But this I have learned: "No Vision, No Passion; No Passion, No Vision." Passion and vision are inseparably linked. Can you articulate what you see in the future for this church? What does it look like? Who attends? What does it value? What makes it different than other churches? Where will it be? What do you see?

Purpose Statements

Begin by writing out a vision and/or purpose statement. Much has been written about vision, mission, and purpose statements in this generation. Quite honestly, I have read so many differing opinions that I become confused. In *Art of the Start*, Guy Kawasaki says it best, "Forget Mission Statements; they're long, boring and irrelevant. No one can ever remember them—much less implement them." This great book for entrepreneurs continues by saying, "Instead of a mission statement . . . craft a mantra for your organization."[3]

Do not get bogged down in the complicated definitions out there. Too much emphasis has been put on crafting a clever statement to impress people. My guideline is: Say it simply and it becomes more powerful. Besides, the painstaking process of developing a purpose statement is more for you than for the people in your church. The process will clarify your own purpose, understanding, and vision for the church. If you need some ideas for writing a purpose statement, research other churches and compile their purpose statements. As you read them, see which ones capture your heart, and make a note of them. Some people have told me not to read anyone else's stuff, to concentrate on being original. In his PDC Conference Rick Warren tells about a guy who declared, "I'm going to be original or nothing." Rick quickly points out that he was both! Sometimes the claim to originality is arrogance in disguise. Many gifted people have gone before us that can serve as a primer for our thoughts. Most purpose statements are a variation of the Great Commission, found in Matthew 28:19–20, and those verses can only be repackaged so many ways.

The Springs did not have a customized purpose statement for three years, and no one in our church ever asked me what it was! We even grew to over 300 people without one. If your church does not make it through the first year, it does not matter how clever your purpose statement is. I have observed churches with a great presentation package, including the vision statement, purpose statement, core values, demographic studies and strategy, fail. Give more time to "people work" than paper work.

Do not misunderstand me; you NEED a purpose statement and all that goes with it, but these elements are more for you and the potential organizations that may sponsor the church. Clarity comes when a church planter writes out a proposal. If the plan cannot be concisely and motivationally written, it has not yet been adequately thought through. Spending the extra hours will give a solid foundation upon which to present God's vision for this new church. Remember that thoughts disentangle themselves when they pass from the lips to the fingertips.

At first, we used one of Saddleback's statements to outline our purpose: "A great commitment to the Great Commission and the Great Commandment will build a great church." As we grew, we developed our own purpose statement: "The Springs exists to be relevant as we lead our generation to God and connect people to a growing community of Christ followers." The shorter statement our people often hear is: "We exist to lead our generation to God." We may say it several different ways, "We want to make it hard to go to hell from Ocala"; "People matter to God"; "Run to the darkness"; "Shoulder up with someone neck deep in sin"; and "It's not about you." Regardless of how you say it, the church's mission is to reach the lost and develop the saved. How you say it is not nearly as important as how effectively you do it.

Strategy

After the purpose statement has been crafted and/or borrowed, develop a strategy to fulfill it. That great theologian Yogi Berra is the one who said, "If you don't know where you're going, you will wind up somewhere else!"[4] Your strategy will get you where your purpose statement is leading. Strategy is the process of fulfilling your purpose. The purpose statement answers the question, "What are you trying to do?" The strategy answers the question, "How do you do it?" If a strategy is too complex, people will not be able to follow it to completion.

The Springs is a purpose driven church, following the Saddleback strategy for making disciples. Our strategy is simply to move people through a series of classes that introduce them to one of our five purposes as a church. In CLASS 101, we teach them what it means to follow Christ and be a member of The Springs, and then we ask them to commit to membership. In CLASS 201, we teach them the habits of a Christ-follower and ask them to make a commitment to pursue those habits in their lives. In CLASS 301, we teach people how to discover their ministry at The Springs, and ask them to sign up for a ministry position. In CLASS 401, we train people how to share their faith and ask them to commit to do it regularly. Classes alone do not make people disciples, but commitment to what they have learned, will. The people who attend all the classes become the foundation and core of The Springs. This strategy also gives us a measurement for effectiveness in each of the purposes within our church.

Core Values

Core values are essential because we only do what we truly believe, and core values help you determine as a church what you should be doing as a result of your beliefs. Resist the urge to have a large list of core values too early on. Take time to research churches on the Internet. Most churches list their core values along with their purpose statement. Compile the core values of other churches and determine which ones resonate with your heart and vision.

The Springs' core values are posted on signs on the walls in the lobby and hallways because what people see, they come to know. The strategy is to weave the core values into the language and lives of our people. There is nothing like hearing members talking to guests and answering their questions with our core values. I once overheard one of our members saying to a guest, "Yes, but here at The Springs we focus on the things that unite us not the things that divided us." In fact, Andy

Stanley, Pastor of North Point Community Church in Atlanta, Georgia asked at a conference, "Is what's hanging on the wall happening down the hall?"[5] A leader must incorporate these values into the life of the church. Teach them, quote them, and speak of them often. Core values are not up for debate; they are the non-negotiables for your church. As an example, the core values of The Springs are listed below:

- "People Matter to God": We Value People
- "Teaching is for Life-Change": We Value Application of Scripture
- "Real Christ-followers Grow": We Value Growth
- "Growing Larger and Smaller at the Same Time": We Value Small Groups
- "God is Honored in Excellence": We Value Excellence
- "Every Member is a Minister": We Value Service
- "Changing Methods—Unchanging Message": We Value Creativity and Innovation
- "Focusing on the Things that Unite Us, Not the Things that Divide Us": We Value Unity and Diversity

Core values must move from being simply a list of statements to being the language of the people. Translate them into easily quotable phrases.

Training

There are more opportunities for training than ever before in church planting. Purpose Driven has been training church planters through conferences for over ten years. Ed Stetzer reports, "There is strong evidence that Basic Training makes a major impact on PDC church plants."[6] Stetzer notes in his study of over 600 church plants that those purpose driven church plants that participated in the Basic Training were substantially larger than those that had not attended training. Below is a chart comparing attendance figures:

	Did Not Participate	Participated in Basic Training
Year One Worship mean	66	46
Year Two Worship mean	60	76
Year Three Worship mean	73	115
Year Four Worship mean	60	198

The *Starting a Purpose Driven Church Regional Conferences* have proven beneficial for our church planters through the years. These conferences are simply the beginning of training for planters.

The results improve when training events are combined with a Purpose Driven Coach. And results continue to be enhanced when a planter joins a network of church planters. When you combine conference training, a coach, and a network of other church planters, you have the winning combination. Purpose Driven offers all three on *www.pdplanting.com*.

Coaching

There are over 10,000 certified coaches in the business world today; it has become a $630 million industry. Most leaders realize the benefits of a proven coach to help them achieve their dreams. If corporate America invests so much to advance careers and financial gain, church leaders should also reap the benefits for eternal investments.

I have personally learned the value of a coach/mentor in my life. The Springs was looking great in 2001. All the charts were going up and to the right. Attendance was at an all-time high of 1,500, giving was healthy, over 200 people were baptized in 2000, but the staff was on the verge of collapse because of the rapid growth. As a pastor, I did not know where to turn. I had never led a church this large, and had no idea how to lead larger. While all the signs were saying growth was continuing, I had more questions than answers, and I felt very alone. Emotionally and physically exhausted, I needed the expertise of a consultant, but everyone I contacted was ten to twelve months out on their schedule. In sheer desperation I e-mailed Rick Warren, outlining our phenomenal growth and all of my fears about leading to the next level. Within a couple hours, Doug Slaybaugh, the Executive Pastor at Saddleback at the time, phoned. After talking for an hour, he graciously offered to come to The Springs and consult for us. Within two weeks, he was on our campus leading us through a changing church. We found we had to restructure our staff, plus hire additional staff to handle the growth. That one consult gave us the knowledge to take The Springs to the next level in growth. Because of my near leadership meltdown in a growing church, I have learned the value of asking for help and have since then used the services of coaches in my ministry.

Starting churches is a team effort. Do not fly solo. During the Dream Stage, invest time and money in all three opportunities of conference training, coaching, and a church planter network. The long-term benefits for your church will far outweigh the short-term financial investment.

---

[1] Wilkinson, Bruce, *The Vision of the Leader*, Global Vision Resources, 2001, p. 11, session 1.

[2] Kouzes, James and Barry Z. Posner, *The Leadership Challenge: How to Get Extraordinary Things Done in Organizations.* (San Francisco, Calif.: Jossey-Bass, Inc. Pub., 2003).

[3] Kawasaki, Guy, *The Art of the Start: The Time-Tested, Barrtle-Hardened Guide for Anyone Starting Anything.* (Portfolio, 2004) 3.

[4] Berra, Yogi, *The Yogi Book.* (New York, N.Y.: Workman Publishing, 1998).

[5] Stanley, Andy, C3 Conference. (Dallas, Tex.: 2004).

[6] Stetzer, Edward J., "An Analysis of Church Planting Process and the Attendance of Southern Baptist Church Plants," *The Impact of the Church Planting Process and Other Selected Factors on the Attendance of Southern Baptist Church Plants, 2003,* **www.newchurches.com,** *http://newchurches.com/public/resources/research/ppt/cp_process_study/ Church%20Planting%20Process%20Study%20for%20State%20Partners% 20revision_files/frame.htm*

CHAPTER 6

Building a
Launch
Team

God does not use a lone individual to start a church; he builds teams to launch churches. As God prepares you, he is also preparing a group of people to start a church with you. Be encouraged that God is speaking to others about being part of what he is stirring within you. The challenge then becomes finding those individuals. The true challenge is when a leader moves into a new city to start a church without knowing a soul in the community. Rick Warren moved from Texas to Orange County, California, to start Saddleback Church without knowing anyone there. His California realtor became the first member he met in the Dream Stage of launching the church. Wherever you start, know that God will be sending people into your life to build the church. Every time you get an opportunity to share the vision with someone or a group of people, watch their responses. It will be clear if God is stirring in their hearts to be a part or not.

Dream	Design	Launch	Development	Strategic Leadership
0–3 Months	4–6 Months	6–8 Months	8–12 Months	1 Year and Beyond

Remember that you are building a launch team not a core group. A core group will want Bible studies and worship experiences. A core group will immediately want to start acting like an established church. There is no church until you launch it. A launch team is focused on the aspects of launching, the assignments, and responsibilities. Their job is to get this church off the ground, and their part is to train and prepare for the launch. A true launch team is focused on inviting and investing in people in their relational world. On the other hand, I have seen too many core groups form, only to turn inward before they ever have a church. They t

One way to start building a launch team is to begin by praying with close friends about the new church. Some of those close friends may even become a part of your church. If I had not asked Jeff Scott, my good friend in Atlanta, to pray for

You can never imagine whose heart God is preparing to help you start the church.

me, he never would have joined me as our worship leader. You can never imagine whose heart God is preparing to help you start the church. I have known leaders who asked friends to pray with them, and their friends then physically moved with them to start the church. Hal Mayer, Lead Pastor of Church at the Bay in Tampa, Florida, enlisted a staff of seven to start the church. Four of the seven staff relocated to Tampa from various cities and states for the church launch. A church planter in one of my coaching networks, Billy Rollins, Lead Pastor of Church @ The Vine in Kissimmee, Florida, moved to the area from South Florida with a launch team of several other couples from the same area. Do not be afraid to ask people to become involved in a new church. Sometimes friends even refer other people who would like to be part of a new church. Meet local church leaders and share the vision. They may have a heart for starting new churches, or they may provide people or prayer support.

Another method of building your launch team is informational meetings. Advertise on a Christian radio station about a new church starting in the area, and invite people to an informational meeting. Use the meeting as another avenue to cast the vision with clarity. The more you cast vision to people, the clearer it becomes.

As you begin building a launch team, meet with them for vision casting and training. If you are going to study anything, take them through the *Purpose Driven Church Conference* on DVD. Focus them on the launch date of the church. Once you tap into one person who is interested in the church, often you tap into several other relationships through that person. Make it clearer and clearer to them. Let the vision capture their hearts the way it has captured yours.

The most effective way for a launch team to capture the vision is take them to see another purpose driven church in your area. Recently, a church starter from Lakeland, Florida rented a bus and brought fifty of his launch team to The Springs for a Sunday service. They scheduled a question and answer time afterwards with our Executive Pastor. It was a huge financial commitment on the leader's part, but most of those people caught the vision. Today this church is nearly three-years old and has over 500 people in attendance.

Tell the stories of life change from churches like the one with your vision. Teach them the purpose, values, and strategy for the church, and you will find you have clarified the vision in the hearts of a young church.

Church planting is no longer a solo sport. More and more, God is raising up church planting teams to start new churches. There are many advantages to starting with a team or staff. One survey of over 600 church planters conducted by Ed Stetzer found that "attendance was demonstrably higher in plants with more than one church planting pastor on staff. The attendance is almost double."[1] The survey also discovered that attendance was increased with two planting pastors, but began declining with three or four pastors on staff.

Other than having someone to share the workload and divide the burdens, another advantage to having a team is an instant camaraderie focused on a central vision. When two church planters link their lives and gifts together, there is often a synergy that advances the church more rapidly into healthy growth. Immediately, more people can be reached for Christ and cared for in the community through multiple leaders. And with faster growth comes faster stability, both financially and emotionally.

One of the greatest challenges of church planting teams is the financial need to launch with multiple salaries. However, once you perform a cost/benefit analysis, many church planters see that the benefits of a church planting team outweigh the costs. First, however, you must decide how to finance God's dream for you.

Financing the Dream

When we started, financing a ministry was my weakness. In seminary, for example, I had the fantastic opportunity to go to work for a great ministry, one that had been the catalyst to disciple thousands of students across the country. After the interview process, I was informed I would have to raise most of my own support. I did not take that position because raising money was not something I was comfortable doing. Many people I know feel the same way. When we began The Springs, I did not even think about asking anyone else for financial support. There was no available denominational support, so we got money from the only other source we knew—our retirement. Teddi and I emptied out

> *Raising financial support will be one of your greatest challenges, but you must learn the art of "the big ask."*

$30,000 from our retirement to begin the church. For obvious reasons, I Do Not Recommend This!

Raising financial support will be one of your greatest challenges, but you must learn the art of "the big ask." No one told me that it was okay to get financial sponsors. It's okay! Dream big and ask big. William Carey, a missionary to India, once said, "Expect great things from God, attempt great things for God." It requires a lot of money to launch a purpose driven church. I am asked often how much money it takes to start. I have seen some guys blow through $500,000 in the first year, and still not have much to show for it. I have also seen some new churches start on $30,000 and do very well. Sample budgets are listed on *www.pdplanting.com*.

The first place to start raising money is an affiliated denomination. Some denominations do a great job financially supporting new churches. Seek out all denominational options first. Contact church planting organizations that support new church starts. When you approach denominations and other organizations, realize that they will require a church master plan.

Next, write a letter outlining the vision for a new church. Specifically spell out starting needs like sound equipment, computers, and advertising expenses. Several examples can be found on *www.pdplanting.com*. Send the letter to everyone you know: churches, denominational leaders, friends, relatives, and ministry associates. Just as you did not know who would comprise your launch team, you do not know who God is preparing to fund this church. Clearly cast the vision, and share the financial need. Big vision brings big support.

Nelson Searcy, founding pastor of The Journey in New York City is a masterful fund-raiser when it comes to new churches. Rather than simply targeting $50 a month per contributor, he mobilizes partner churches to form a team of support. He casts big vision for reaching a big city with big needs requiring big money. Nelson focuses on the presentation of the vision to a potential partner church, not simply a slick marketing package. This technique goes back to passionately casting the vision, rather than simply packaging the vision. We must be able to personally share the vision in a manner that excites and *hooks* potential financial backers. The Springs is one of their partner churches. Nelson reminded me that I never saw any piece of material about Journey before committing to support them. I was hooked by Nelson's heart and vision, and it was credible because I knew other leaders who supported him. He has modeled the power of networking. Once he secures a partner church, he asks what other church leaders they know who might have a heart for New York City. People with a heart for starting new churches know other people who have a heart for starting new churches.

The Dream Stage will be a roller coaster of emotions for the church starter. As I mentioned before, the highest thrills and the lowest frustrations will be your partners in the early days of a church start. Some days you will come home exhilarated by God's provision through people and circumstances, other days you will race down the hill of depression in the darkness of the tunnel you just entered. Be encouraged because, like a roller coaster, the climbs take longer and are more exciting, and the falls come quickly and are over sooner. Sometimes you will feel like the wheels came off the car and you are in a free fall. During the free falls, keep your hands reaching for heaven. Know the One who invited you to join him and strapped you into his work of reaching a community for Christ. He who called you is faithful. When you come through the biggest drops of starting a new church, he will be there, asking you if you want to go again. Buckle up and enjoy the ride!

---

[1] Stetzer, Edward J., *"The Impact of the Church Planting Process and Other Selected Factors on the Attendance of Southern Baptist Church Plants,"* Ph.D. Dissertation, The Southern Baptist Theological Seminary, 2003, 21.

CHAPTER 7

Lessons from the Trenches

There is nothing more disconcerting than being awakened in the middle of the night by a nightmare. It seemed so real. Your heart is still beating uncontrollably, and you are breaking out in a cold sweat. As you look around the room you realize everything is okay. You are safe. It was just a bad dream. Go back to sleep.

Many pastors experience the same symptoms one year into a new church. They dream about a new church that will impact their generation and community. They dream about hundreds of people finding a relationship with Christ, creating powerful God-anointed worship experiences that will fuel a community of Christ-followers to live with a passion for God. They dream of a place where broken people are made whole. They dream of a church that is a healthy, growing, vibrant work of God.

But one year into a new church start, they realize that church was just a dream, and the church they are leading is a nightmare. What could they have done differently?

Dream	Design	Launch	Development	Strategic Leadership
0–3 Months	4–6 Months	6–8 Months	8–12 Months	1 Year and Beyond

Let me share some lessons I have learned in the trenches of starting a church.

Lesson #1: Love Everyone but Move with the Movers

Some of the greatest counsel Rick Warren ever gave me was "Love everyone, but move with the movers!" In the first year of starting The Springs, Teddi and I taped this motto on our bathroom mirror, because everyday we needed to be reminded of it. With the early uncertainty of a church plant, we felt we could not afford for anyone to leave the church. The truth we soon learned was, we could not really afford for everyone to stay.

For example, about six months after starting The Springs, a leadership team member challenged our strategy for having seeker sensitive worship services. He believed the church was a place for believers and the worship service should be fully-oriented around them. He believed

We determined a core value of The Springs was that people matter to God—lost people matter to God.

evangelism was for outside the church, not inside. This man had faithfully loved me and prayed for me. He had encouraged me in the lonely and challenging beginning days of the church. His vision, however, did not line up with what God had called The Springs to be. Soon after that meeting, he left the church. *Love everyone, but move with the movers!*

Had I caved into someone else's view of the church, I would have missed The Springs becoming a vibrant place for the unchurched to attend. We chose early on to become an outwardly-focused church. We decided to make it hard to go to hell from Ocala, Florida. This decision meant I could not please my close friend. We determined a core value of The Springs was that people matter to God—lost people matter to

God. They were welcome at The Springs; more than that, we designed our place for them. By holding firmly to this core value from the early days, thousands of people have come to know Jesus Christ. Once your core values have been set, you must be willing to take bullets for them. Be unshakable in your resolve to protect and implement your values.

Next was the couple who had been in a certain type of evangelism training. They believed in knocking on the door of every visitor and presenting the gospel to them. They had been trained that this was the only proper method of evangelism. It violated The Springs' decision not to invade the private lives of our visitors, allowing guests to anonymously kick the tires of Christianity. This couple loved Jesus and served him faithfully. Yet they could not understand not invading people's personal lives to share Christ. They left The Springs. *Love everyone, but move with the movers.*

My heart does beat evangelism, and I love to train people to share their faith. Years before, I had been a certified trainer in the form of evangelism they wanted me to pursue. And in a strange way, I felt I was violating my own evangelistic heritage. I wrestled with whether or not I was watering down the gospel message by not doing evangelistic visits. I had been taught that relational evangelism was for weak Christians. And because we focused on relational evangelism, public invitations in our worship service were contrary to our vision. I realized early on that the only people who came forward were church people. Lost people did not want to walk forward in front of a couple hundred people they did not know, to meet a man they did not know, to be introduced to a God they did not know. We give people an opportunity to receive Christ at their seats and record their decision on a Communication Card. Does it work? Over 300 people every year have committed their lives to Jesus. Sixty percent of our members have given their lives to Christ at The Springs.

Then there was the man who loved everything The Springs represented as a church. As we grew, our music developed an edgier worship style. We never sang hymns, but he loved hymns. He grew up on them. They moved him to worship. He loved the teaching; he just could not stand our music. The music was too loud, the songs lasted too long, and he did not like to stand for the entire worship set. He was a gifted teacher and even taught our CLASS 201 for a season. He was, and still is, a good friend. He left the church. *Love everyone, but move with the movers.*

There is nothing that defines a church more than its music. Your music will determine who you reach and who you repel. So clearly define your target and do not veer off course. We have had some people say we must believe God is deaf, because the music is so loud. Others have said, "If it's too loud, you're too old!" And I agree. Our focus is, and always has been, the next generation. If we had given in to some very dear friends who love hymns, our church would have missed the younger generation. I grew up singing hymns. Some of them still ignite my heart with worship for the Father; however, I learned long ago, and remind our people often, that it is not about you and me anymore. It is about the people who are not here yet. Our music will continue to define us.

It is somewhat easy to move with the movers. Where some church planters fail is loving everyone. It is easy to discard those who disagree. I have witnessed many pastors who leave a high body count in their path. They bulldoze over people who oppose them, instead of loving them. I love each of the people I have written about. I

- - - ➔

Love indiscriminately. But chase hard after God's dream for your church with the movers he has placed on your team.

◀ - - -

just did not surrender the leadership of The Springs to them. To this day, I have a good relationship with each of them.

Love indiscriminately. But chase hard after God's dream for your church with the movers he has placed on your team. Rick Warren also taught me to never surrender the leadership of the church to whiners. I never have, and I never will. As a young church planter with little self-confidence, those words gave me courage to lead confidently and to tenaciously pursue God's calling for my life. In the early days of a church plant there is incredible pressure to compromise the vision God has given you. Because I held firm to my vision, it only took about eighteen months for all the people who helped us begin the church, but who had conflicting views, to leave. We lost dozens, but gained hundreds.

Lesson #2: Don't Surrender the Vision

There will be people along the way who will challenge you to surrender the vision that God has given you. Do not surrender it. In the early days, there was a couple who fell in love with The Springs. They loved the fellowship, the teaching, and the worship. They served tirelessly in ministry. They could always be counted on to give their best. We loved them and their children. After attending Saddleback's *Purpose Driven Church Conference*, I implemented the Purpose Driven DNA at The Springs. The church was six-months old and running around 120 people. The couple quickly challenged this "new vision," insisting that the church should follow their vision as well as mine. He openly challenged me, saying my vision was not the only vision for the church. Even then, I knew that vision was all I had. God instilled in me a passion and a vision for building a church to reach the next generation. Vision was my bridge to the future. I reminded my friend that he did not leave his job and step into financial insecurity to begin a new church. For him, church was somewhere he attended; for me it was the calling of my life. I ate, slept, drank, and breathed The

Springs. As my friends left the church, The Springs was more and more God's fresh work in my life. It was there that I saw God move and demonstrate his power. It was there that faith became reality.

I am confident that the pastor is the visionary leader of the church, and you cannot create vision from consensus. Surrender the vision to other voices and the church will quickly become a diffused powerless institution. Lead with God-given vision and the church becomes a laser light-focused agent of life change.

Don't surrender. Lead.

Lesson #3: Accept Everyone Who Walks in the Door

Acceptance does not mean approval. Create an atmosphere of acceptance. In the early days, when we were meeting in an old theater, a guy walked through our doors. He was far from God, and in fact, he was an atheist, living with a woman, but walked in because somebody had been badgering him to come to church. When he showed up, he was wearing ripped jeans, had multiple tattoos, studded wrist bands, long earrings, a Grateful Dead bandanna with skull and crossbones on it, and a leather jacket. He walked in daring somebody to talk to him. Guess what happened because we built this atmosphere of acceptance? People warmly welcomed him, poured coffee for him, and said, "Come on in, man. We're so glad you're here."

He came back the next week. They called him by name, and he found acceptance. Then God started breaking down the barriers. Four weeks later, he gave his life to Christ. He called me after he gave his life to Christ and said, "Ron, I don't have anyplace to live. I've been living with a girl, and I know that's wrong, so I need to do something about that. But, now I'm homeless."

I said, "I need to pray about that."

I hung up the phone, and God said, "What do you need to pray about? You've got a place here. He can come and live here. Give him the keys."

He moved in and lived upstairs, and we watched God transform him. He went on to lead ministries in our church and led many people to Christ.

Remember, just because you accept them, it does not mean you have to approve of their lifestyle. And, just because they are different, it does not make them unworthy of your church. Be unflappable when people come to you. You have no idea what they have been through and how they have lived. And you have no idea what God wants to do with them.

Lesson #4: Realize the Impossible is Always Possible

Take your dictionary off your shelf and cut out the word "impossible." It does not exist.

You can look up the word "impossible" in my dictionary and it isn't there, because I've cut it out. Because I know all things are possible with God. I challenge you to do the same. Take your dictionary off your shelf and cut out the word "impossible." It does not exist. I have seen too much at The Springs. Miraculous things happen everyday.

We were moving into our third location as a church, the Castro Theater. We were six-months old and it was the first time we had to pay rent. The facility needed a lot of renovation, but we did not have any money. I calculated that we needed $18,000 to do the renovations and pay rent through the summer. Our offerings were running about $1,000 a week at that time with 150 people. This moment was a test of my leadership in our young church. I challenged that small group of people to give $18,000 on one Sunday. We called the offering, "Find Us Faithful." It was Memorial Day weekend in 1995, and I asked people to come forward and lay their gifts on the stage. After the service, we had a covered dish lunch at the church while a group counted the offering in the back room. There was electricity in the air and incredible excitement among our people. I walked into the back room where they were counting the money. I had never tried to raise money before; I had no idea what was going to happen. If we did not get the money, we would have been finished. We would have been another church statistic—another failed church start.

I asked the counters, "Guys, did we make it?"

One man turned around and had tears just running down his face. "Yeah, we made it."

I said, "How much?"

He said, "$50,000."

In one week, 150 people gave $50,000 in cash.

Then he said, "You've got to see this." He held up one check for $25,000, with no name, no address, and no phone number on it—just initials.

We had no idea who it was, but we knew who sent them. God has said to me, "You be a risk taker. You trust me for the impossible, and I will do it." The exciting thing is, you will see that over and over again in your church. Trust him. God is ready to take care of his dream.

Lesson #5: The Revolving Door of the Core

There is a principle somebody taught me early on, the principle of scaffolding. When you build a building, scaffolding goes up. When the building is done, the scaffolding comes down. God uses people in the process of building a church. Some people are only there for a season. And when the season is over, they are gone. Some people are scaffolding that God uses to build the church. I would not encourage you to call your people "scaffolding," just know it exists.

A young church does tend to be more transient than an established church. As a pastor, you need to learn how to say hello and goodbye. Leading a rapidly growing church is like preaching to a parade. God sends some people just for a season. Enjoy the season. They do not all leave because they are unhappy with the church. Some do, but not all of them. Some will not like the church to grow beyond a certain size; others will not move to a new location; some will take job transfers. The reasons vary, but the result is the same. People come and people go. Hold them loosely. Trust the fact that God is the one that builds his church.

Lesson #6: Starting a Church is a Family Affair

Church starting is a family affair. It is not simply an entrepreneurial endeavor that you pursue by day and come home to your family by night. This calling involves your entire family. If you are married, the calling is on both husband and wife. Teddi and I were called to start The Springs.

In the early days, Teddi did everything. She was the name tag person. She was the potluck coordinator. She coordinated the 101 Membership classes. What I did not have time to do, she did. We were a team. Rick Warren's wife, Kay, said something to pastors' wives at the 1995 *Purpose Driven Church Conference* that really set Teddi free. She said, "First of all, be yourself. Also, realize there's maybe not just one ministry God has called you to as the spouse of a pastor. You are called to be flexible and to be willing to move in and out of roles." That message gave Teddi the courage to begin a children's ministry although she had never done anything like that before. After all, we needed something for our own children.

The early days of a church require the entire family to participate. Cherish those memories together. Our boys, Jared and Jacob were seven- and nine-years old when we started the church. Our nine-year-old's job was just to change the transparencies on the overhead projector. I had a business card printed for him with the church logo and his name on it. He was my intern, and loved it. He carried that card in his wallet. Jared and Jacob went with me to church before the services and they set up chairs and put out worship guides. They were there to clean up after the services. But you know what? It was *their* church.

Church starting is also an adventure. The exciting part for our family was praying together for God to provide everything. When we started the church we needed a sound system. The four of us prayed, and God provided a sound system. Two weeks before our first service we visited Teddi's parents' church in Tennessee. I sat next to a man in the back of the church who had no idea we were starting a church or had been praying for a sound system. In the course of our brief conversation he said, "You know, I bought a sound system a year ago, and I really wanted God to use it. I thought God wanted me to buy it, and the church used it once last year. I'm really kind of ticked about it."

I just looked at him and asked, "Well, how badly do you want God to use that sound system?"

He said, "What do you mean?"

I told him we had been praying for a sound system because we were starting a church. He said, "Meet me here tomorrow morning. We'll pack it up and you can take it with you. Use it as long as you need it."

It was a twenty-four channel board with a hundred-foot snake, monitors, microphones, and cables. It was more than we needed—and it was free. Our boys watched their faith become fact as we loaded that sound system in our van. Church starting really is a family affair. Do not cheat your family out of an incredible spiritual growth experience.

Your spouse is critical in the birthing of a church. Often we have seen church starters go home from a conference with excitement about starting a purpose driven church, only to be met with opposition from their spouse. For this reason, we encourage spouses to attend our conferences. Teddi spends time with wives, challenging them to discover their own calling in this new church venture. Starting a church is a discovery process that must involve agreement of the husband and wife first, for it will be an all-consuming endeavor. If your mate is not on board, your marriage will suffer. Without the support of your family, the church is almost certainly doomed to failure. If the family isn't behind the vision, then God is telling you the time is not right to start a church. He is not necessarily saying, "No," he is simply saying, "Not yet."

Lesson #7: His Grace is Always Sufficient

> ---->
> *Whatever awaits you in the days ahead in starting a church, you will find his grace to be sufficient.*
> <----

We have found God's grace to be powerfully strong. It carries you when you cannot walk alone. Whatever awaits you in the days ahead in starting a church, you will find his grace to be sufficient. After four and a half years, and moving from one rented location to another, we settled into location fourteen for The Springs: a vacant grocery store. Our original plan was to throw some walls up with minimal work and use the facility for short-term use. Soon the project took on a life of its own. It skyrocketed to a $700,000 renovation of 34,000 square feet. There were 400 people at The Springs then, and we had to do the majority of the labor. We could not afford to hire a construction company, just a contractor to oversee our volunteers. The project would take nine months to complete, and I had to lead the charge to raise $700,000 in one year and challenge our people to build it themselves. The project seemed impossible. (Refer to Life Lesson #3.)

We called our campaign "The Run Home," because it was going to be a semi-permanent place for our church, with the hope of purchasing the entire shopping center in the future. At about this time, I was at a conference with our staff and I started getting dizzy while driving. When I went back home to see a doctor I was diagnosed with a brain tumor. I remember lying in the MRI tube, praying. I don't know if you've ever been in an MRI tube, but there's not a lot to do in there. God and I were talking.

He spoke very clearly and said, "I'm going to use this, son."

At that point, I knew there was something wrong with me. When I came out of that tube, a friend of mine who is a neurosurgeon was there. He was talking to Teddi and some of our close friends about the brain tumor. He knew the kind of tumor, and he knew a specialist in Tampa that could remove it. In the entire state of Florida, this surgeon specialized in the removal of this rare form of brain tumor, and my friend just happened to have served his internship under him. God had orchestrated the whole thing. The timing could not have been worse for a brain tumor, but I guess the timing is never good for that. I had to lead the charge to raise $700,000 in order to begin construction on the facility, and in the meantime, was diagnosed with this tumor.

Everything was progressing fine, until the tumor encroached on my optic nerve and my right eye locked, necessitating an eye patch for the duration of my illness. The day finally came to see the doctor in Tampa one last time before surgery. Simultaneously, I was preparing for the start of the church construction and kind of in denial about the surgery. I thought, *Okay. We'll get through this. I'll be out in a couple weeks and back in the church.*

That day, the doctor sat down and gave us all the bad news.

He said, "Ron, even though the tumor is most certainly benign, it is located in a very bad place at the base of your brain." And then the litany of probable side effects began. "You need to know that your voice will never be the same. As a matter of fact, the tumor is wrapped around all the nerve endings. Your eyesight might not come back. You're probably going to have facial paralysis like a stroke victim. You're going to have to learn to swallow and eat again because of the nerves that are impacted. Best case scenario—you will be out of the pulpit for up to six months. Worst case scenario—you might want to find another line of work."

I said, "First problem—we don't have a pulpit. We have a music stand. Second problem—you've got three weeks. I have to lead." Our doctor was a strong follower of Christ, and he just smiled at me. I'll never forget going home that day. Teddi and I drove home to Ocala from Tampa in total silence. I was not ready for that news, and I did not know how to handle it.

The day of the surgery arrived. We had so many people praying. My neurosurgeon friend was in the operating room with us, and he said he had never seen anything like it. Normally, with this kind of tumor, they have to pick away all the nerve endings because they wrap themselves around the tumor. But, when they went to cut it away, the nerve endings literally peeled away from the tumor. They simply pulled it out.

The doctor said, "At that point, I knew that there would be minimal damage." To us, it was minimal. The only thing I lost was everything associated with my right ear—the ear drum and ear canal. Three weeks after surgery, I was sitting in a chair in the worship service with a patch on my bandaged head teaching and leading. The entire time we had many young believers on their faces praying for their pastor. When God told me that day, "Son, I'm going to use this," he meant it. Our people rose to "The Run Home" challenge, with 400 people committing $712,000 in one year. By the end of the year, they had actually given $750,000 over and above regular tithes and offerings. They built the place themselves. I watched God meet every need. As always, he carried us.

I do not know what you will face. But, I know who's going to sustain you. Here's the key. Don't dare let your daily time with God falter. Do not just buy into a good process on which to build a church. Lock in your time with him, and let it be fresh every day. You need his power, his strength, and his wisdom. We can give you all the plans, but they are worthless without him. You will find that his grace will be strong and powerful in your own life.

Stage Two

Design Stage

- Designing a Purpose Driven Church
- Leadership and Administrative Structures

Dream	Design	Launch	Development	Strategic Leadership	
0–3 Months	4–6 Months	6–8 Months	8–12 Months	1 Year and Beyond	

CHAPTER 8

Designing a
Purpose Driven Church

Ny son, Jacob, worked in the concrete business one summer for a member of our church. It was backbreaking work and I was proud of him for sticking with it. Every day he would come home filthy and exhausted. He would spend the entire day forming the foundation of a building with rebar and wood framing. It was important for the form to be just right before the concrete was poured, because after the concrete was poured into the form, it was only a matter of hours until the foundation was set. If it was not formed correctly, the crew would have to come back and sledgehammer the entire foundation. Failures in formation are painful and expensive. The same is true in starting new purpose driven churches. The future shape of a church is set by the form cast in the early days.

It is crucial to design the right form before people start pouring into that form. The form a leader constructs will shape the future of the church. Do not take the beginning form of your church lightly. The future of a church is formed by its

Dream	Design	Launch	Development	Strategic Leadership
0–3 Months	4–6 Months	6–8 Months	8–12 Months	1 Year and Beyond

worship style, teaching style, leadership structure, and its heart for people.

Determine Your Worship Style

More churches split today over worship style issues than theological issues. Therefore, it is crucial for the leader to decide early on what style of worship they will embrace. Keep in mind, worship style is not simply musical style. The entire worship experience from music to video to spoken word must be evaluated through the eyes of the people you are trying to reach. When you confidently determine who your focus group is—who you are trying to reach—it makes crafting a worship experience for *that person* so much easier. Through some trial and error, you will learn what works and does not work for your target group.

In the early days of The Springs, the services felt more like a family with only around 100 people attending. During that season in the life of our church, we built a greeting time into the worship service. We encouraged people to greet everyone, not just the people seated next to them. Our people were shaking hands and hugging one another. It usually took about five minutes to get everyone back into the flow of the service.

Although our people loved it, our guests hated it, because they were outsiders. I saw nothing wrong with our style of greeting until I watched it affect a friend of mine. I had been building a relationship with this guy for two years and sharing Christ with him.

> *The worship service must be designed by thinking of how those far from God will respond.*

Finally, he started attending The Springs. Then I noticed he missed several weeks, and I asked him where he had been. He told me he really enjoyed the service, but the greeting put him on edge. He just was not comfortable with strange people in his space. So he left the church. That was it. I knew then that part of the worship service had to change, although our people loved it. They were used to it, but we must never forget who we are trying to reach with the gospel. The worship service must be designed by thinking of how those far from God will respond.

The Style of Music Will Define and Shape the Church

The most important factor in defining and shaping your church is the style of music.

Music has become as controversial as theological differences between denominations. Music is almost a denomination of its own today in the church culture. When you read a denominational sign on a church you know what "style" they are. When the first song cranks up in a worship service, you know what style they are. A church's musical style will define your church in the community, so choose your music carefully.

Choose the style of music that attracts those you are attempting to reach. Research what music they listen to throughout the week. Rick Warren discovered this by taking a survey of his congregation during the beginnings of Saddleback Church. He asked the congregation to write the radio station they listened to most on their communication cards and place them in the offering. He discovered the overwhelming majority of his church listened to "Top 40" radio stations. So Saddleback chose a style of worship music that was similar to that sound.

Hymns will not reach people without a church background. The struggle over traditional hymns and the music of today has ushered in an era of "worship wars" in full swing in churches and denominations. Many churches are changing their style of music to "contemporary worship." The problem is, everybody defines contemporary worship their own way. I have been in churches where "contemporary" meant 1970s praise choruses.

For other churches "contemporary" means a blend of secular music and Christian rock songs.

The bottom line is we need new music to reach a new generation. This concept is nothing new. Psalm 40:3 (NCV) says, *He put a new song in my mouth, a song of praise to our God.*

The easiest way to define your music is to look for some model churches that are reaching your target and use their music. See what churches like Saddleback, Fellowship Church, Willow Creek, and North Point Community are using. They have already done the research for us. The laboratories of worship are the churches that have gone before us. Learn from their discoveries. As you grow, your church will continue to grow and evolve into your own unique style.

Do Not Try to Reach Everyone

Rick Warren uses the illustration of the radio station that played all different types of music—rock 'n' roll first, then jazz, some rap, and then easy listening. How many listeners do you think they had on that radio station? NONE! They did nothing but frustrate and confuse people. Churches today are offering multiple worship venues with different styles of music in each. When starting a new church you do not have that luxury; the goal is to just get *one* service off the ground.

Focusing your music on those you are trying to reach will not eliminate others from the mix. It is interesting to see the different people we attract who are not our focus group. At The Springs our music style is anything but traditional. What has been interesting is to watch how many senior adults come to The Springs. Our music is loud. Since my brain tumor surgery, I am deaf in one ear, but it is loud even for me. Because they love to be around life and changed lives, some of our senior adults walk into the worship center and turn off their hearing aids until the music is over. They say, "It's not my style of music, but I love seeing people come to Christ and their lives changed forever."

It's interesting to note that older people will tolerate the music of younger people more than younger people will tolerate the music of older people, as long as they are exchanging their musical taste for seeing people come to know Christ.

Your Music Will Determine Who You Will Keep and Who You Will Lose

Music will determine who you reach, and who you repel. Music has the power to define a church. As a leader, you need to be okay with people leaving or staying at the church because of the music.

There was a man in the early days of The Springs whom I loved dearly. He was a teacher, passionate about seeing people grow in their faith. I loved him, and he loved me. He enjoyed everything about The Springs except our music. He asked, "Ron, why don't you throw a hymn in every now and then?" I replied, "No. There are some great churches in town that are doing hymns. You can go to one of those. This is who we are."

To this day every time I see him around town, he tells me he never should have left The Springs. He still has not locked into another church but he continues to invite people to our church, even though he left. Music defines who you keep and who you lose.

Determine the Balance between Performance and Worship

As you begin you will need more performance-based music in your services, since it is more intimidating and uncomfortable to sing with a smaller crowd of people. Remember that during the early days of a new church, everyone is unfamiliar with the music and flow of the worship service. Ask yourself, would you like to sing out loud with a small group of people you do not know? When you do sing congregational songs, make certain the volume of the music is up high enough to drown out individual voices. Having a vocal team will help, as opposed to a solo vocalist.

Find a balance between worship and performance. Some churches sing worship songs for forty-five minutes. Generally, people new to church do not want to worship for forty-five minutes. They are unfamiliar with the concept, and besides, they do not know how to worship. They end up watching you worship for forty-five minutes, which is far too long. Unchurched people are more comfortable watching performance music than watching believers worship for long periods of time. Keep them in mind when planning the music.

Determine the Length of Service

The pastor has to determine the length of a service. Be brutally honest with yourself—it needs to be a lot shorter than you want. Today's generation wants everything fast. They get everything fast. From video *clips* to sound *bytes,* everything is short, fast, and succinct. MTV and VH-1 have shaped the attention span of an entire generation. We have *fast food, drive-throughs,* and *pay-at-the-pump.*

At The Springs, our service is sixty minutes long. You can cover a lot of ground in sixty minutes. It's all a matter of crafting a worship experience where everything ties together. Planning will be the key, and we will look into it in the Development Stage.

You have to determine the worship style. You have to lock in unapologetically to who you are trying to reach and do not veer off course. You will have many people trying to influence your worship style. If you let them, there goes the vision of the church.

Develop Your Teaching Style

Right now there is a generational shift taking place in how pastors preach in churches. Outdated styles of communication are not producing life change.

Pastors are communicating with a previous generation. We have been taught to present information—not to teach in a way that transforms lives.

George Gallup said, "Never has the gospel of Christ made such inroads into the church with making such little change in the way people actually live."[2] While we live in an information age, we have not learned what to do with that information.

Since the Word of God does not return void, the Word of God is not the problem. The way we communicate is the problem. We have forgotten to interpret the truth using this generation's language. It is not about the wrong message; it is about the wrong presentation of the message.

Several years ago, Teddi and I were given a gift certificate to Ruth's Chris Steak House, a very exclusive restaurant. Everything was perfect—the atmosphere, the service, the food presentation, the food itself. The server cooked our food table side and taught us how to cut the meat. Gingerly, the food was placed before us. When Teddi rose from the table, our server quickly took her napkin and folded it, neatly placing it on her seat. We could not take two sips of water without our glasses being refilled. Everything about that place centered on the service. That same steak could have been served in another steak house, and it would not have been as good, simply because of the atmosphere and presentation.

In many ways, we are serving the same spiritual steak with very different results. We must remember we are serving a new generation. Often times in a church, the unchurched are not left wanting more, but wanting out. We are to be head waiters of God's Word to this generation. First Chronicles 12:32 (NIV), says, *The men of Issachar,* **who understood the times and knew what Israel should do** (emphasis added).

In the same manner, we must emulate the men of Issachar and understand the times we live in.

Purpose driven teaching results in life change, not information exchange. Purpose driven teaching always precedes purpose driven churches. We must learn to communicate to this generation first, before we start churches to reach this generation. If you carry your old communication style into a new church, you will have an old church. The communication style of the teacher is the first identifying mark of a purpose driven church. We must learn to communicate more than just mere information.

Let me illustrate the information vs. communication dilemma. A few years back, Teddi and I were white water rafting down the Ocoee River in Tennessee. We were with a group of students and we were each on different rafts. Teddi's raft went down the river, through some very difficult rapids. On one run, Teddi was thrown out of the raft into the raging rapids. There were Class IV rapids just down river from them.

If you have been white water rafting, you know what to do when you fall overboard. The guide trains you to come up looking for a lifeline. If you are close to the raft, the guide will extend the handle of his paddle to pull you in.

This scenario did not go as planned. Teddi did not come floating back to the surface. She went under water, her foot wedged between two rocks, and she could not get loose. She could not get up and was trapped under the water. The guide spun around looking for her to come back up out of the water, and she did not come up.

Teddi later said she saw her life flash before her under the raging rapids of the Ocoee and she thought, *this is it, I'm done.* As she relaxed, it was as if someone took her foot and just twisted it and moved the rock. She came bobbing up to the surface, and gasped for breath. Heading straight for the

Class IV rapids, Teddi was trying to catch her breath and did not know the danger she was drifting toward.

A highly-trained professional guide took his paddle and screamed at her, "Teddi! Do you know the original Greek for paddle? Do you know the historicity of the paddle?"

Of course not! He did not say that! He said, "Grab the paddle!"

A whole generation is gasping for air and headed for Class IV rapids. Sometimes all we offer them is an explanation of the Greek and Hebrew. They are looking for a lifeline, not information. They need someone to throw them the lifeline of truth, not a Greek lesson.

People struggling to save their marriages do not really care who the Hittites are. But they desperately want to know how to communicate with their spouse again. They want to know how to forgive their spouse and how to fall in love again. God wants the same things in their lives, so he put those answers in the Bible. The pastors of this generation must learn to speak the language of this generation. Are we preaching to impress seminary professors, or preaching to change lives? Rick Warren says, "The Bible determines our message, but our target determines when, where, and how we communicate it."[1] Purpose driven teaching is about applying the Bible to this generation. Howard Hendricks has said, ". . . interpretation without application is abortion."[2] Truth must come alive in individual lives. If we teach merely Greek and Hebrew lessons with biblical history sprinkled in, we have failed to teach for life change. Application of Scripture is the act of breathing life into this generation. Jesus emphasized the doing of the word, not just the knowing of it. Consider John 13:17 (NIV): *"Now that you know these things, you will be blessed if you do them"* (emphasis added). And Matthew 7:26 (NIV): *"But everyone who hears these words of mine and does*

> *The pastors of this generation must learn to speak the language of this generation.*

not put them into practice *is like a foolish man who built his house on sand"* (emphasis added).

I challenge every church starter to watch Rick Warren's *Preaching for Life Change Conference* on DVD. (It's available at *www.pastors.com*.) It will challenge you to think and teach differently. The conference revolutionized my teaching. People may criticize this style as "shallow teaching" or teaching to meet felt needs. My study of Scripture reveals that is exactly what Jesus did—he met the felt needs of people. In churches we have defined preaching one way, and anything different is suspect.

One Sunday a group of potential church starters came and observed our service. After the service, one man was looking around and asked, "So when do you teach the Bible around here?" Now mind that he had just sat through one of my messages in a worship service. I knew what he was getting at, so I asked him, "Do you mean when do we teach the Bible the way you are accustomed to hearing it taught?" The message I taught explored about fifteen verses of Scripture. I spoke to him at length on why and how we teach for life change. He did not like my answers and I am sure he regretted asking. Teaching for life change stretches everyone.

Since changing my teaching style ten years ago, our people report that they understand the Bible for the first time in their lives. "I get it!" is not an uncommon sentiment. Others thank me for making the Bible so easy to understand.

The mark of a good teacher is to say complex things simply. Take deep truth and make it seem easy. Put truth on the lowest shelf, so everyone can reach it. As we read the Scriptures of Jesus teaching the multitudes, we see him teaching culturally relevant messages. He talked in parables we have to reinterpret for this generation, because they do not necessarily understand biblical culture and context. We need to teach modern day parables in today's context . . . Just as Jesus did 2,000 years ago.

---

[1] Warren, Rick, *The Purpose Driven Church: Growth Without Compromising Your Message & Mission*, (Grand Rapids, Mich.: Zondervan, 1995), 159.

[2] Hendricks, Howard, *Living by the Book*, (Chicago, Ill.: Moody Publishers, 1993), 284.

CHAPTER 9

Leadership and Administrative Structures

Decide on Your Leadership Structure

Everything rises and falls on leadership. The leadership temptations in the first days of a new church are one of two thoughts. One temptation is

> *Everything rises and falls on leadership.*

to put together a leadership structure too soon with boards, positions, and policy. Another temptation is to fly solo with no accountability. Both extremes are dangerous for a church starter, because both accountability and counsel are essential. Take the time to develop a leadership structure that accomplishes both.

Move Slowly

Move slowly when choosing the leadership structure for a new church. Do not feel like you have to have the entire structure in place in the beginning. As a matter of fact, it works

Dream	Design	Launch	Development	Strategic Leadership
0–3 Months	4–6 Months	6–8 Months	8–12 Months	1 Year and Beyond

better if you don't hastily throw the leadership structure together. If you choose the structure or the leaders too quickly, you may have a painful mess to clean up.

Resist the urge to move quickly, and methodically set a structure. If you are in a denomination that has already chosen your structure, then move slowly in choosing the leaders within the structure. The challenge in a new church is not really

. . . the leadership of a church sets the tone for the spiritual maturity of a church.

knowing the people. I chose our first team much too quickly. If I could do it all over again, I would wait nine months to a year before I gave anyone a leadership position. Enlist people in ministry, but do not give them leadership authority in the church too quickly.

Church Leaders

Beware of asking community leaders to be leaders in the church. Obviously, being a leader in the church is totally different than being a leader in the community. I have seen churches place some of the most worldly bank presidents on the finance team. They certainly had financial knowledge, but not spiritual maturity. Community leaders may be ego-driven and spiritually bankrupt. Church starters fall into the trap of thinking a community leader in church leadership will be great for the church. It could be disastrous. Be very careful not to quickly give preference to society leaders in your church.

Many could be great leaders. But place them there first for their spiritual maturity you have seen and second for their expertise, not the other way around. Keep in mind that the leadership of a church sets the tone for the spiritual maturity of a church.

Godly Servant-Leaders

As a new church begins, find your leaders among those who serve. Look first for the people who are willing to clean toilets and vacuum the church.

Surround yourself with godly servant-leaders who own and understand the vision of the church. I always had a circle of men who served as counselors and a sounding board. There were some seasons when I did not give them a title. I just asked them to meet and pray with me. All of these were men I had met serving in the church.

I learned this principle of looking for servant-leaders in the first nine months of The Springs. We had been meeting in an old theater, and it had to be cleaned often. We had Saturday workdays, and one Saturday morning we were scrubbing mildew off of the top of the outside of the building with bleach and rubber gloves. Working beside Bruce Gaultney and James Duff led to lifelong friendships. Bruce was the editor of the newspaper in town, and James was a CEO for a hospital in town, but I did not know it at the time. I did not care what they did for a living, all I knew was they were willing to scrub mildew off the top of a building for a new church with 120 people in it. The kingdom is comprised of leaders who serve. Find people like Bruce and James, and surround yourself with them.

Conversely, beware of people who come to a new church and ask to be in leadership. Tell them to grab a vacuum or clean a toilet. Jesus' model of leadership was that of a servant-leader. In Matthew 20:28 (NLT) Jesus said, *"For even I, the Son of Man, came here not to be served but to serve others, and to give my life as a ransom for many."* Jesus came to build an upside-down kingdom, where the greatest would be the servant. His church is to be led by servants. Find people with servants' hearts who own and understand the vision of the church.

The very first leadership team I put together, I put together too soon. Some did not own the vision—they loved God—but they miscued on the vision. The truth is, we were still trying to figure it out ourselves. But when the course was set to be a purpose driven church, several could not line up with it. Within two months, all of them left. That entire team left the church, and in the last ten years, only one person has ever asked me where they went.

Simple and Flexible

Place people in ministries, not meetings. Do not set up a leadership structure that has many levels and committees. Streamline it, and keep it simple.

Sometime in the first six months of The Springs, I e-mailed Rick Warren a question about leadership structure. He referred me to his seminar on tape called "Simple Structure," and it was precisely what I needed. In it, Rick challenges pastors to keep the structure flexible. (To purchase this tape, see the Appendix for information.)

What works for 100 people does not work for 500, and what works for 500 people does not work for 1,000. The skeleton must be able to grow or the body cannot. The leadership structure is the skeleton of the church body. Keep the structure simple and flexible, because it is going to have to grow with the church. If you lock the structure in, and say, "This is the way we're doing it," you will stunt the growth of the church, and you will structure the church for control instead of growth.

We can see this principle by looking at our kids' toys. The simple toys like blocks and tinker toys do not break as easily as the complex toys. Simple is usually more durable, and the same is true for church leadership structure. For example, one church I consulted with had 180 leadership positions in their bylaws, but the real problem was there were only 150 people in the church! Streamline the leadership of the church for effective ministry. Remember, less is more.

Administration

If you are a typical church starter, the word "Administration" is much like the sound of fingernails being dragged across a chalkboard. Administration may not be high on your spiritual gift list; however it is required in the church. I know . . . you are a big-picture person, a communicator, a risk taker, not a bean counter! Word of warning . . . someone had better be administrative in your organization. And the buck stops with you. Here are a few random thoughts from a non-administrative person about administration in the early months of a church.

Quickly develop some financial accountability systems for the church. The best place is through a mother church. They already have those systems in place and could handle the limited needs of a new church fairly easily. Church at the Bay in Tampa, Florida, is one of our church starts this year, and we are handling all of their financial systems until they can establish the administrative teams necessary. This method provides confidence in your financial systems for new people in the church. There is also a comfort level in knowing that you are not handling your finances alone.

Some simple financial thoughts:

(1) The pastor should NEVER handle the offering.

When people attempt to give you their offering, direct them to the ushers or administrative team.

(2) Use two signatures on each check.

This builds in a system of checks and balances, offering financial accountability in the church.

(3) The pastor should not be the signer on a check, if possible.

If that is not possible, never sign a check written to yourself.

(4) Have at least three respected people count the offerings.

(5) Alternate the counting teams so as to rotate different people each week.

Avoid using the same teams together, and do not use husband and wife teams. This is all in an effort to stay above reproach in the area of finances.

(6) Use an offering count sheet.

Keep accurate paper records of cash offerings and checks broken down on the counting sheet.

(7) Make copies of deposited checks.

(8) Deposit the offering as soon as possible.

If you do not have an adequate safe, use the night depository at your bank. Many banks will allow you to come in the next day and count the offering.

(9) Keep good records of individual's contributions in a database program.

During the first year of The Springs, we did not keep adequate records. We lost much of the first twelve months of financial history. A church can keep track of contributions through good database software. There is a good selection of software on the market today. Church Growth Software actually has a Purpose Driven Module that is very user friendly, *www.churchgrowthsoftware.com*. For accounting software, QuickBooks® is excellent for a new church. It is reasonably priced and fairly easy to use. As the church grows, you will need to upgrade to other programs, but these two programs are an effective way to start.

The biggest challenge in the financial area is how to build financial accountability when you do not have people yet. And even if you do have people, who do you trust? Trust three people on your launch team to be the administrative team.

Choose people of high integrity and financial aptitude. Choose people who are heart deep in the church, which means they are tithers. They are not decision makers, but they provide financial accountability. They count the offerings, record the contributions, deposit the offerings, and write the checks. Another option is to obtain the services of a CPA firm in your area. Many firms will offer services to churches in order to provide financial accountability.

Incorporating the church is another administrative step to be taken care of in the Design Stage. Hire a local attorney to take care of the incorporation, and the establishment of a 501(c)(3). You will need the 501(c)(3) in order for people to receive tax deductions for their contributions to the church. There are many way to incorporate online today, but I would encourage you to utilize the professional services of an attorney. It will cost you more on the front end, but you will have confidence that the legal process is handled correctly.

Let's move on to why you are in this: the people.

Stage Three

Launch
Stage

- Launching a
Purpose Driven Church

Dream	Design	Launch	Development	Strategic Leadership
0–3 Months	4–6 Months	6–8 Months	8–12 Months	1 Year and Beyond

CHAPTER 10

Launching a Purpose Driven Church

Twenty years before we started The Springs, my aunt and uncle lived in Titusville, Florida, near Kennedy Space Center. The Apollo rockets were launching during this time. When a launch was scheduled, they had to remove everything that was hanging on the walls because their house shook so violently. An Apollo rocket was not only seen for hundreds of miles, but it was felt by everyone within a thirty-mile radius.

Like an Apollo rocket, purpose driven churches are launched into communities. They explode onto the scene and capture everyone's attention.

To start, a launch team is formed during the four-month launch period and they partner with other churches for a big launch day for their new church. A marketing plan is developed, the service is planned, and teams of people are enlisted or borrowed from other churches. On opening day the goal is to have a fully functioning team and hundreds of first time guests show up for the service.

Dream	Design	Launch	Development	Strategic Leadership
0–3 Months	4–6 Months	6–8 Months	8–12 Months	1 Year and Beyond

Rick Warren says in his *Purpose Driven Church Conference,* "I've noticed over and over that if a church doesn't get beyond 200 within about a year and a half, it usually doesn't happen at all. On the other hand, churches that get over 200 in the first year just keep on growing and growing."[1] The goal of a launch is to attract a crowd and develop the crowd into a church.

The foremost reason for launching a new church as large as possible is simply good stewardship of the gospel. All evangelism is based on extracting from the community at large those people who are seeking God. The term "seeker" is becoming outdated in our church culture; however God is very interested in "seekers," since God is the one who creates a "seeker," as defined in Scripture:

> *"No one can come to me unless the Father who sent me draws him . . ."* (John 6:44 NIV)

By gathering as many seekers as possible in one place, we maximize the impact of the living Word of God. The Word of God is the Sword of the Spirit that God uses to pierce men's souls.

> *For the word of God is living and active. Sharper than any double-edged sword, it penetrates even to dividing soul and spirit, joints and marrow; it judges the thoughts and attitudes of the heart.* (Hebrews 4:12 NIV)

Therefore, every time the Word is shared, all seekers within earshot are potential converts. The larger the seeker crowd, the more potential impact of the Word of God.

Launching large is congruent with the best of missionary theology and with the methods of Jesus. Everywhere Jesus went, he attracted large crowds of people, all potential converts for his redemptive plan for their lives. We are called to do the same in our generation.

While coaching dozens of church starters through the Launch Stage, I have observed several benefits to launching a church large. First, a church launch breaks through growth barriers more quickly. There are invisible barriers at certain sizes in every church. It seems as if there is a lid on the church's growth that cannot be removed. One of the most effective ways to shatter the barriers is with momentum. Momentum is one of a church starter's best tools for growth. A train that is stopped on railroad tracks can be kept immobile by a block of wood strategically placed on the track in front of the train. However, a train moving at eighty miles per hour on the same track can shatter a brick wall. The difference in the two situations is momentum. Launching a church large produces tremendous momentum.

Credibility is another benefit of launching large. One of the greatest challenges for the leader of a new church is credibility. When we started The Springs, we had very little credibility in the eyes of new guests because we were small. We also were meeting in portable facilities, which give the appearance of a temporary church. People would come in and wonder if we would be there the next week. I was not a proven leader. But what gave me greater credibility was the growth of the church. Proverbs 14:28 (MSG) reads, *The mark of a good leader is loyal followers; leadership is nothing without a following.* When a church grows, it gives the leader credibility in the eyes of people attending. When a first or second time guest walks into a new church and sees 200 people, he immediately senses that something good is going on. The leader must be doing a good job, and this begins to establish credibility in people's eyes. Conversely, when guests walk into a two-year-old church, and there is only a small group of people worshiping together; leadership comes into question.

The third benefit of launching large is that the church can become self-supporting faster. The Springs was week-to-week in our finances for years. Several times the church had to hold our paycheck in order to pay other bills. Not being trained in starting a church, we did not know how to raise financial support. And so, The Springs had to be self-supporting from the start. Many church starts live on life support from financial supporters for years. In most cases, if a church cannot become self-supporting in two to three years, they never will. By initially attracting a large crowd, the church has the ability to quickly break growth barriers and financially care for the needs of a growing church.

Financially, it costs a lot more to launch a church. A church does not get a chance to ease into the costs associated with start up. You will need to rent or purchase equipment for the worship service and children's ministry. A sound system, video equipment, computers, lights, band instruments, and children's nursery supplies are all essentials. On top of this list, you will need a way to transport and store all of the equipment. Marketing the launch is a large financial commitment. Printing a mailer and saturating the community with direct mail is expensive. Presently, we spend about $5,000 to print and mail a 40,000 piece mailer. Depending on the mailers you send, you could spend up to $10,000 just for the mailer.

Launching large will also cause you additional stress and criticism. Since you do not get to ease into the growth of the church, you will have to begin leading a church of 100 or more. With that growth comes the stressful challenges of learning how to assimilate and develop people. Criticism from others is the unexpected price any church starter pays. When we began the church, I was taken back by the criticism that came from other churches. I had a difficult time imagining how a new church could possibly be a threat to anyone. Each time we moved to another location, a church in that area would complain that we had moved into their neighborhood. Rapid growth is suspect to some churches who have not experienced growth in decades. They often will attribute your growth to the suspicion that you must be teaching "easy believism" or that you could be a cult.

When speaking to church starters in the *Purpose Driven Church Conference*, Rick Warren often says,

> "When you are small, they will dismiss you. When you are growing, they will criticize you. When you are big, they will resent you. So don't pay any attention to them!"[2]

Pastors have a propensity to become "defenders" of their point of view when they are criticized. Do not mix it up with critics. Stay focused on the work God has called you to do for him. As Rick says, "If you wrestle with a pig, both of you will get muddy, but only one of you will enjoy it."

Preview Services

One of the most significant new discoveries in starting churches in the last decade is Preview Services. Preview Services are much like previews for an upcoming movie. After winning a newspaper competition at ten years old, I was invited to the preview of a new John Wayne movie called *The Cowboys*. It was held at Radio City Music Hall in New York City, and John Wayne himself and the entire cast were going to be there. As I walked into the theater there was an excitement in the air. I even got the opportunity to see a movie that had not been released to the public yet. Likewise, Preview Services introduce the community to a new church that has not been released to the public yet. Previews are not abbreviated versions of the church. At Radio City Music Hall we watched the entire movie, not

Previews give a church time to build momentum while providing a chance to test-drive the facility and the service you are designing.

an edited version. At a Preview Service, the community is invited to see what the church will be like at the Grand Opening.

Previews give a church time to build momentum while providing a chance to test drive the facility and the service you are designing. It is similar to the soft opening of a restaurant; when they invite friends for a test run before opening to the public. There are many variables when it comes to setting up a new facility with new equipment, not to mention new people, since everything is new, and everyone is inexperienced. Previews also give your team the opportunity to get some experience under their belts. While you do Preview Services, the momentum builds over a period of four months. The typical strategy is to have three preview services, one a month. On the fourth month, the church has a Grand Opening service. Launching a new church used to be a one time event. Preview Services are just the beginning of the Launch Stage and they give the church an opportunity to build a crowd before the Grand Opening.

Previews, in addition, allow a church to build a critical mass of people for the new church before launching. Would you rather walk into a new church in town and be greeted by a room full of empty chairs and twenty people, or a room filled to capacity with 200 people? Guests prefer to remain anonymous and "kick the tires" on a new church, and it is difficult to remain anonymous in a room of twenty people. If a room is three-quarters empty, it does not have the critical mass it needs to provide a safe environment for guests. Each Preview Service is designed to build on the previous one. The goal is to always have more people at the next preview. This growth continues to build momentum and excitement among the people as the Grand Opening approaches.

As the pastor, you will want to make sure the room is full for Preview Services and Launch Services. A full room will require a lot of hard work for you and your launch team. First, ask your launch team to make a list of ten people they are going to bring to the services with them. After they have made the list, ask them to give it to you. One week before the event call each of them and ask about every person on their list. Pray for each of those people by name. If you have twenty-five people on your launch team and each brings ten people, you have a crowd already.

Enlist temporary workers from other churches. Ask sponsor churches to commit a group of their people for the Preview Services and Launch Services. This enlistment accomplishes two things; one, it takes the stress off your launch team to do all the ministry that day, and two, it fills the room. Recently we had 150 people sign up to be on church launch teams for two churches we started this year. These teams take care of the setup and breakdown, children's ministry, greeters, ushers, and parking ministries. Locate some churches that may not be as able to give you money but can send mission teams to help get the church launched.

During the four-month launch period, continue to train the launch team, and meet with them weekly. After each Preview Service plan a comeback event for the visitors. A comeback event is not a big event but an opportunity to connect people who have attended a Preview Service. It is designed as a smaller gathering allowing more personal interaction with people as they take next steps toward the church. Invite them during the Preview Service to come back in two weeks for a party or picnic or any type of social gathering. Comeback events are also great opportunities for people to meet the staff. At every comeback event the pastor must use some time to cast the vision for the church. Also at the comeback event make sure to invite them to the next Preview Service, and even give them an opportunity to serve in some capacity. Remember, people are looking for two things in a church—relationships and responsibilities. It is also important to have printed information about the church available for people to take home.

Following is an example of a typical Launch Schedule:

June 15	Preview Service
July 1	Comeback Event
July 15	Preview Service #2
August 1	Comeback Event
August 15	Preview Service #3
September 1	Comeback Event
September 15	Launch—Grand Opening of Church

Marketing the Church

Without marketing, a new church will struggle to come into existence. It is more and more challenging to capture the attention of people in today's society. Some of the most effective advertising we had in the first year of The Springs was free advertising. At our first Easter Service, several people gave their lives to Christ. Among them were a man named Ed and his wife. I talked with the group after the service about baptism and explained that as soon as we found a place to baptize we would call them. Ed spoke up and said we could use the family-owned springs called Blue Grott

As we walked down the stairs into the fresh water springs, there was a natural wall of green foliage surrounding the area. It made for a beautiful backdrop as people followed Christ in baptism. The baptism service was planned for a Sunday afternoon, and our church was so excited. We baptized fourteen people, worshiped together, cooked out, and enjoyed what God was doing in our young church. Without my knowledge, someone had called the newspaper about our baptism service. Since there were a lot of people taking pictures that day, I did not know until the next morning that one of those was a photographer from the local newspaper. As I grabbed a cup of coffee and sat down

In each community, different forms of advertising work better than others.

with the morning paper, I was in awe. There on the front page of the *Star Banner* was a picture of me baptizing a young woman. The headline read "Baptism at The Springs." We could not afford or obtain advertising like that! Market your church by notifying the local newspaper of what you are doing as a new church in town.

In addition, you will need to learn the advertising culture of your community. In each community, different forms of advertising work better than others. For some communities, newspaper is the best advertising, in others, it is billboards, and in others radio or direct mail. Without knowing your community, it is difficult to say which form of advertising is the best for starting your church. Direct mail is one method many church starters attempt first. Direct mail, however, does not usually work in large cities that are direct-mail saturated.

We partnered to start a church in New York City in 2002 called The Journey. Direct mail is ineffective in the city, so the lead pastor, Nelson Searcy and his team had to be creative in getting the church's name out. They practiced servant evangelism with teams standing in front of office buildings in the financial district of New York City passing out breakfast bars with a postcard about the church stapled to them. In an hour they handed out nearly 5,000 breakfast bars. They did the same thing with bottled water on hot days. A church starter has to creatively assess the culture God has called him to reach.

For instance, in Orlando, Florida, direct mail is not effective for new churches. Mailers are sent out to homes almost weekly advertising some new church meeting in schools or theaters. The challenge is, many of the mailers appear to be junk mail and are tossed before ever being read. Marketing companies report an average return of .5% on your mailer, meaning if you mail a 40,000 piece mailer, you should expect 200 people to come to your service. I personally have never seen that happen. The reality is probably closer to .25% return.

If you live in a direct mail saturated community, you will need to get creative. My brother-in-law, Joel Wilson, started a church, The Church at Lake Conroe in Houston, Texas. They are in the shadows of a megachurch that uses direct mail and has over 10,000 people attending. To get a bigger response, Joel sent out a mailer that was black and white. The front of the mailer was solid black with their Web site address in white letters. The back was information about their church launch. He also rented several billboards in the area using the same simple Web site message: black billboard with white lettering. His Web site received 600 hits the first week. They had over 100 new people show up for the first service.

Direct mail is still one of the most effective methods for marketing the church when done properly. There are many companies that offer direct mail marketing to new churches and existing churches; you can find a list in the Appendix at the end of the book. Whether you design the mailer yourself or use a professional, do it with excellence. Remember that direct mail is a first impression, and you only get one chance to make it good! Saving more money on a substandard mailer may result in saving less people in your community. There is a lot to learn about the direct mail process, and for that reason I would recommend using a direct mail service. At the least, recruit some help from a church who has successfully used direct mail.

A church start shared with me their own horror story of having spent thousands of dollars for a direct mailer and not having a single person show up. After being asked to review the mailer, I was not surprised by the lack of response. There was no date on the mailer. People were invited, but not at any particular time, and there were several misspelled words.

A mailer must be an attention grabber that appeals to the felt needs of your target audience. Design every aspect of the mailer to capture the attention of your focus group. Promote message topics that are going to hit where they

- - - ➤

Be willing to take calculated risks in marketing your church.

◄ - - -

live, such as: stress, relationships, finances, success, marriage, family, anger, and anxiety. Make the mailer easy to read with plenty of graphics and white space. If the mailer makes it past the two-second garbage sort in the hands of the recipient, there is a better chance they will come and visit.

Be willing to take calculated risks in marketing your church. Some of our advertising lessons have been painful ones. Often new churches tend to overanalyze their target market and hurt their outreach effort. Previously, we had a community event for our Children's Ministry and premiered one of the new VeggieTales® movies. We put our advertising money in a direct mailer and radio advertising. A local Christian radio station came and did a live remote on site, where we had blow-up rides for the kids, food and drinks. We sold out five shows and had over 2,100 people attend, with many of them visiting our church afterward. Two years later we did it again, but this time we "targeted" the unchurched. We went with secular radio, not Christian radio. We had 500 people show up. Essentially, we reached no one new. Too often, we forget the advertising power of Christian radio and the religion section of the newspaper. Unchurched people looking for a church still look in the church section or listen to Christian radio. For that reason, we advertise weekly in the church section of our paper.

Our local newspaper has worked well for our marketing needs in Ocala. Once, we advertised in the movie section with an ad that looked like a movie ad. The headlines read,

"If you like *Sister Act*, you will love The Springs!" We had one line reviews from some of our members, and it proved to be very effective.

However, advertising must not oversell and under deliver. Another time we ran an ad among the bar ads in the paper. It featured a picture of our band and read, "Live Band. No Cover Charge." We used that to kick off our new Saturday night service. When I stepped up to teach that night after the music, a group of people got up and walked out. They were there for the band. While it was a cute church ad, we misrepresented who we were.

A church starter must know the community. Take a lesson from corporate America on this one. The average McDonald's® owner/operator knows more about the community culture than the average pastor. McDonald's owners and managers are actively involved in their communities, and pride themselves on giving back to their communities. Ray Kroc, founder of McDonald's said, "We have an obligation to give back to the community that gives so much to us." McDonald's considers it their corporate responsibility to be active in education and youth development, local sporting activities, health care efforts, and disaster relief. McDonald's is well versed in the needs and activities of their community. The church must do the same and keep up with the culture that we are called to reach.

When we partner the eternal message of Christ with the best marketing practices of our day, we can launch a church that will shake a community like an Apollo rocket.

Marketing will make the launch an exciting one. In today's marketing-savvy culture, we must learn to be excellent communicators of God's church to a world whose vision has been dulled by sensory overload. Every day they are bombarded by slick graphics, photos, and video images seeking to capture their attention. The secular world uses full-color marketing and expensive presentations to represent and sell products that are temporary. The church has *the* product that is eternal. When we partner the eternal message of Christ with the best marketing practices of our day, we can launch a church that will shake a community like an Apollo rocket.

[1] Warren, Rick, *Purpose Driven Church Conference*, Saddleback, 2004.

Stage Four

Development Stage

- The Development Stage
- Developing the Worship Experience
- Installing the Purpose Driven CLASS System
- First Year Ministries

Dream	Design	Launch	Development	Strategic Leadership
0–3 Months	4–6 Months	6–8 Months	8–12 Months	1 Year and Beyond

CHAPTER 11

The Development Stage

W hen I was a kid in the 1960s, my first camera was a Polaroid®. I had never seen anything like it. Miraculously, the picture developed instantly, right before my eyes. Back then, in order for the picture to develop properly, a coat of something had to be smeared on it. If I got in a hurry and did not take time to prepare the picture properly, it was underdeveloped. The picture was not a total loss, but it was not all it could have been either.

Churches often do not take the time to develop correctly. As a result, they miss the full evangelistic potential God has planned for them in their community. Underdeveloped churches also struggle to present a clear picture of the church to a lost world today.

The Springs is eleven-years old and is *still* developing. A growing church is always going to be tweaking and improving.

Dream	Design	Launch	Development	Strategic Leadership
0—3 Months	4—6 Months	6—8 Months	8—12 Months	1 Year and Beyond

The church starter's task is to tenaciously create environments that partner with the Holy Spirit to effect life change.

One of the first environments that we must continue to develop in new churches is "The Lobby."

Developing a Lobby Experience

The tendency for new churches is to work overtime on making their worship experience the best it can be in rented facilities and with borrowed equipment, all the while trying to appear professional on a shoestring budget. The one environment in the church that is highly overlooked is the lobby. But as the first point of contact for a new guest, it is the first impression. A great lobby needs a "wow" factor to let the guests know they are in for a treat during their visit. The lobby for a church is the entire weekend experience: from parking to foyer to bathrooms to children's ministry to café to worship service. The lobby is an all-encompassing experience for a guest.

When you visit a first-class resort, it is obvious more money is spent on the lobby than on the rooms, for they understand the value of a lobby as a first impression. Teddi and I stayed at Gaylord Palms Resort, in Orlando. Walking into the lobby was breathtaking—high ceilings, opulent chandeliers, expensive artwork lining the walls, the staff greeting you as you enter. "Welcome to Gaylord Palms. May we assist you? Can we take your bags? May we wipe your nose?" Okay not that last line, but it sure felt like they would have done it if I asked! The lobby flows into the hotel atrium. The ceiling opens to a massive room filled with foliage from around the world. At the top of the ceiling is a beautiful glass dome, allowing you to look into the sky as you walk around the hotel. Everywhere you walk, uniformed staff is ready to serve. It is apparent they have been highly trained to serve their guests and attend to their needs. You feel comfortable and important at Gaylord

Palms, because they have created an environment in the lobby that warmly welcomes their guests.

Contrast that experience with the average church in America. After searching for a good parking space—for what feels like an eternity—you make your way toward the church. The building has dozens of doors and you are not certain which one to walk through. As you enter, there is a sea of people. No one speaks to you or welcomes you. You are not sure which way to go to the worship center and you search tirelessly for some sort of signage. Where do you take your children? Where are the bathrooms? After you finally find a seat in the worship center, you notice everyone else around you has a worship guide that you somehow missed. You get up once again and find a stack of them in the corner that all the "regulars" are picking up. Before the service even starts, you have promised God if he gets you out of here, you will not come back!

What is the difference in the two facilities? In the hotel, care and training were given to create a warm lobby atmosphere. Many new churches, however, do not focus on preparing the lobby atmosphere. Yet it requires a lot less work than crafting a worship experience. As pastors, we must train our people to create a warm and inviting environment for our guests. What church starters tend to forget is that a new church can be more effective at certain tasks than an established church. It is easier to begin with a friendly atmosphere than to try to change an established pattern. Creating a sense of family and acceptance is really much more challenging as your church grows. Therefore, take advantage of the early days and develop the lobby environment. A term I used for our church when we first started was "Faith Family." I taught messages on it and addressed the church by it. We *were* a faith family. Capitalize on your assets as a young church and build a "Faith Family" atmosphere that all starts in the lobby.

How to Build a Lobby Atmosphere

Look through a guest's eyes

What are *they* seeing? Walk through your facility, whether it is a theater or a hall, a community center, or a school. Imagine you are a first-time visitor. Try to see through the eyes of a visitor. It is much easier to do this when you first start, because you are all visitors. Remember, you never get a second chance to create a first impression. According to Barna Research, more than 70% of all people who visit a church make up their minds about coming back before the pastor even gets up to speak. We must create an atmosphere that allows people to be relaxed enough to take steps toward God. Our lobby environment helps to remove barriers people have about church and Christ. There are some key areas to consider as you look at your church.

Visible signage

People walking into a new church are a little apprehensive. One way to help set them at ease is to have visible signage. Start by placing signage in the parking lot. Have you arranged first-time guest parking spaces out front? Is the entrance clearly marked with a banner or sign with the church logo? They should be able to find everything without having to ask. Signs for the nursery, children's ministry areas, worship center, and bathrooms are essential. Look at your entire facility through the eyes of a guest. Regardless of age and size, a church should continually evaluate their signage and direction as a first impression.

I recently attended worship services at one of the largest churches in the country. I was amazed at how difficult it was to find the entrance to the church. I saw it; I just could not get near it. The parking experience was like a maze of cones and entrances and men in fluorescent jackets. Had I been a first-time guest, I probably would have driven away in frustration. Clearly mark your parking and building. Now, contrast that experience with another large church I have visited. As we entered the campus, signs welcomed us, asking first-time guests to turn on their headlights to be directed to parking. I felt wanted immediately as I came on the campus. The feeling of acceptance began with a sign a half mile away from the church.

Background music

Have you noticed as you walk in the lobby of a resort or mall, there is always background music playing? It sets the tone for the experience. During Christmas season, Christmas music is playing throughout the mall. In a resort, instrumental music prepares you for a relaxing stay. Music fills the air and sets the mood for your experience. Music can have a calming effect on the guests at your church. Be sure to choose music they would enjoy. Do not play elevator music if you are trying to appeal to younger generations. The wrong choice of music can send the wrong signal as well. Music in the worship center before the service begins should be similar to the music of the church. I walked into our worship center one weekend and someone had put in music that sounded like a Gregorian chant; not our style of music. The CD was *quickly* removed from our selection. Monitor your music selection. And remember, silence is loud.

Refreshments

Offer coffee and refreshments to your guests. Drinks and refreshments help build a comfortable environment. There is something about giving people refreshments and a cup of coffee that just sets them at ease. This is an excellent ministry for someone to start up in a young church.

Decide whether to offer the refreshments for free or to set up a café. Everyone loves Starbucks® or Barnes & Noble®. Why? Because they invite you to come in and sit. Coffee bars create a feeling of community, breaking down walls and allowing people to stand around and talk. You can chat with a friend or stranger. We receive many compliments from our first- and second-time guests about The Springs Café. It is always packed and has grown with the church. We now offer an assortment of food and drinks. Because most of our guests have never seen a café in a church, they are pleasantly surprised when they see this welcoming environment.

Worship guides

Station greeters to offer everyone a worship guide. Let your worship guide lead guests through the experience, and make it simple but professional. A high-quality worship guide that is well thought out speaks volumes to first-time guests. No one wants to attend a church with poorly presented material, it reflects on the entire congregation. I have a standing joke with my good friend, Judi Lowther. Judi has been a part of The Springs since the early days, and she knows I am a perfectionist. She also knows the stress and frustrations we faced starting the church. During those seasons when I was falling apart on the inside and stressing out about all the details, she would look at me and say, "It may be falling apart on the inside, but it looks good on the outside."

Regardless of what is going on behind the scenes, you have to look good on the outside for your guests. A professional worship guide will help project a positive image. There are companies who specialize in helping produce a quality worship guide. Initially, you might have to pay a little bit more, but they do the hard work for you. There are worship guides with professional graphics on the outside and a blank inside for you to customize.

Include in the worship guide:

- A welcome from the pastor. Describe your church to the guest and welcome them.

- Instructions about childcare and note taking for the message can be a standard blurb.

- Announcements. Use the worship guide as a tool to promote upcoming activities and ministries.
- Communication cards
- Message notes

The worship guide is the written presentation of the church to your guests and will be the only piece of information they take home with them. Take the time to present the church well.

Think comfort

Historically in America, church has been a place we get dressed up to attend. We must intentionally create comfortable environments on the weekends and throw out the dress code because America does not get dressed up for much anymore. Casual dress is "in" for our generation. Some people do not go to church because they do not have the "right clothes." We sent a 40,000-piece mailer to residents of our community recently inviting people to come as they are. A lady wrote and reprimanded me for not making people dress up to meet their Savior. I hope she realizes Jesus meets her at her bedside every morning, even *before* she puts on her makeup. Scripture teaches that God looks at the heart, not the clothes.

Many weeks, first-time guests at The Springs can be a dead giveaway—they wear coats and ties. I have never worn a tie on the weekend, because casual dress sets people at ease. Even my teaching style is casual—I often sit on a bar stool next to a table. We want people to feel like they are having a conversation with an old friend. Comfortable environments remove barriers for the unchurched. They are not as impressed by suits as they are by the honesty of a group of people seeking to follow God just as they are. We must choose to work on hearts, not appearances.

Design a strategy for greeting guests

This might sound simplistic, but you really have to be nice to people when they show up. A friend visited a church start to see how they were doing. He said, "I walked in and nobody said hello to me. I had to look for a worship guide. Not one person spoke to me." The people in that church start are having a good time right now—but their guests are not coming back because there is no intentional strategy in place to welcome them.

Many churches in the country, including us, learned to greet people using Saddleback Church's example. If you go there, you will see lines of greeters as you approach the building. Prior to Saddleback, I had never seen that in a church. These people were smiling and patting me on the back and shaking my hand. By the time I reached the worship center door, my hand was shaken seven times and I was excited to be there because I felt they wanted me there. I had not even seen anything in the church, but the greeters' enthusiasm was infectious.

Greeters should be strategically stationed throughout your facility. Once after eating lunch at the Rain Forest Café in Orlando, Florida, I entered the bathroom and was surprised to see an employee greet me. This greeting location is not recommended for churches. Since I did not walk in there to socialize, it was a little weird having someone greet me in the bathroom, but strangely I felt welcome there. After I washed my hands, he handed me a paper towel and offered me cologne. Of course there was a large tip basket strategically placed on the counter, but you can leave that out at your church. The point is the hospitality industry understands the importance of friendly faces strategically greeting their guests, and the church needs to learn this concept.

Greeters are the key to creating a lobby atmosphere among your guests. Find people that match your target and put them at the front doors. This is important because when people walk in the door, they are looking for somebody that looks like them. And, if you are trying to reach young families in their 30s or 40s, that is who you want out front. Select people who project warmth. Train them how to greet people and what to say. Give them breath mints. Station them in positions and teach them not to huddle up and talk to each other. This is not fellowship hour, it is ministry time. Don't just say, "Go out there and shake some hands." That does not work. They will have a tendency to clump up over in a corner and wind up talking to each other, while all the guests are coming in untouched. Once again, give them stations. Give them positions. Give them breath mints. Have I said that already? Give them breath mints. Teach them to smile. Do not put grumps out front. Do not make the mistake of thinking, "Anybody can do this." There are some people who project a look you do not want to project. Greeting is not really their gift. God loves them, but they have another ministry in the church.

> *. . . when people walk in the door, they are looking for somebody that looks like them.*

Learn the Art of "Chairology"

For a church starter the set up of chairs in the worship center can make or break a worship experience—no kidding. Once you have found a meeting place, practice setting up the room before you begin worshiping there. Here are a few lessons from the "professors of chairology," and while they may seem simplistic, the room set-up dramatically affects the tone of the room.

Set up fewer chairs than you need

As the church fills up, you want to be pulling chairs out from the back room as people enter looking for a seat. It gives new people the appearance that the place was so packed they were pulling out chairs! Never have enough chairs set up in the room.

Avoid a center aisle

Center aisles are great for weddings, but not a worship experience. If you have a center aisle in the worship center, you are preaching to an aisle, not to people for most of the service. Have a full center section of chairs. Place the aisles on the sides of the center section.

Curved, not straight

Curving rows around the front of the room give it warmth and personality. Straight rows seem sterile and institutional. Curved rows also take up more space, which you probably have in the early days of a church. Remember, a room can be filled with 100 chairs or 300 chairs, depending on how the room is set up. Place enough aisles in the room to allow easy access to the seats. You do not want people crawling across fifteen other people to get to their seat.

Space rows comfortably

Walk through the rows and see if you have enough room to pass comfortably. It is not good form for a guest to be squeezing between rows and bumping the back of someone's head with a rear end. This creates an uncomfortable feeling for both people involved, the bumpee and the bumper.

Use Name Tags

We have used name tags for eleven years at our church. As you enter the worship center, station a name tag table with greeters there. As people enter, ask them their first name and handwrite a stick-on name tag for them. People usually will not feel awkward about it because everyone in the church is wearing one. Rarely, guests prefer not to have one, and that is okay.

Name tags allow everyone to be called by their name. As a pastor, there is nothing like being able to call people by name on the first visit. Because it warms up the environment of the church, we ask our people to call everyone by name. This is a lesson we need to learn from the old *Cheers* television sitcom. As their theme song goes, everybody wants to go to a place "where everybody knows your name, and they're always glad you came." We even instruct our worship teams to wear them on the stage.

. . . there is nothing like being able to call people by name on the first visit.

Some of our members have also discovered a marketing strategy using their name tags. People often forget to take their name tags off, and go to dinner or lunch in the community. It is great free advertising for the church. We have had our people tell us they leave them on and people ask them, "The Springs? What's The Springs?" It gives them a chance to invite people to church. Name tags create an environment of warmth and family. The larger you grow as a church, the more you will be inclined to give them up. Hold on to them as long as you can. We are over 3,000 people now on the weekends and still using name tags, because they play a large part in building a community.

Communication Cards

The communication card, which appears on page 138, is not just a card to gather guest information for your database. A communication card is the barometer of what is taking place spiritually in your service each weekend. *It is* the gauge for how successful your church is in reaching people for Christ and teaching them.

When we began The Springs I really did not see the card as being that important for our regular attenders and members to fill out. In my mind it was a guest registration card. I was taught at the *Purpose Driven Church Conference* to have every person fill one of these cards out every week in your service, members and attendees. I walked away thinking, *That's really nice, but I think that's redundant. What about our poor people who, every week, have to fill out a communication card. They're not going to do that. We'll just get the guests to fill them out.*

Then six years ago we began to understand why these cards are important. Most people were not completing them, because they didn't want to take the time to fill out all the information. But we realized that these cards are a spiritual barometer of what is going on in the lives of our people. This is where they would record any spiritual decisions they had made, or sign up for classes, or write prayer requests, or ask for information, or express a need in their life. So, we scheduled forty-five seconds to a minute during the service to fill out the card. During the welcome time in the service, we now hold up the card and say, "Welcome to The Springs. These cards are really important to us. We want to ask everyone in the place, whether you have been here for years or today is your first time with us, go ahead and fill this out." Then the band plays a little instrumental number for one minute. This allows everyone to fill out the information on the card at the same time.

We found that when we gave out pens and gave people one minute in the service to fill out the cards, our responses for Christ went through the roof. People accepting Christ simply had to check a box on the card and place it in an offering bag. Our responses from first-, second- and third-time guests went through the roof. Baptisms went through the roof. Prayer requests sky-rocketed. Just because we gave them one

minute in the service to fill it out. I am a firm believer now
that you must monitor the spiritual heartbeat of your people,
and completed communication cards accomplish this task.
If for nothing else, but the prayer requests we receive as a
result, it would be worth it. We have much more knowledge
concerning the needs and hurts of our people through their
written prayer requests.

Then on Monday morning we have a team of volunteers
who input the data on the cards into our Church Management
Software, taking most of the day to complete the task. After
everything is entered, reports are generated and e-mailed to
the appropriate staff and ministry leaders for action.

Once people have made it through the lobby, they have
name tags, they have been welcomed, and there is coffee and
refreshments. Your people have been friendly but not
overbearing. The visitor is thinking, *I'm okay. This is comfortable,
warm and safe.* The whole time you have been knocking down
their barriers as you have created this inviting atmosphere.
Now it is time for the worship experience itself.

Communication Card

☐ New address   Date _____

PERSONAL INFORMATION

☐ Mr. ☐ Mrs. ☐ Miss ☐ Ms.

First Name: _____

Last Name: _____

Address: _____

Address 2: _____

City: _____ State: _____

Zip Code +4: _____

E-mail: _____

Home Phone: (___) _____

Office Phone: (___) _____

Mobile Phone: (___) _____

Please indicate: ☐ Single ☐ Married ☐ Widowed

Date of Birth: _____

How did you hear of us?

☐ Newspaper Ad ☐ Friend ☐ E-invite
☐ Direct Mail ☐ Other

_____

_____

I am a: ☐ Member ☐ Attender
        ☐ 1st time ☐ 2nd time ☐ 3rd time

Current School Grade? _____

Names, grade and birth dates of family members who attend:

Mr./Mrs.	Grade	DOB
Mr./Mrs.	Grade	DOB
Mr./Mrs.	Grade	DOB

My decision today:

☐ I'm committing my life to Christ for the first time
☐ I want to be baptized
☐ I'm renewing my commitment to Christ

I'd like information on:

☐ How to begin a relationship with Christ
☐ How to join this church family
☐ Home Teams
☐ Student Ministry
☐ Children's Ministry
☐ Celebrate Recovery
☐ Nearlywed/Newlywed Class
☐ New Believer's Class

I'd like to serve in the . . .

☐ Preschool Ministry
☐ Children's Ministry
☐ Student Ministry
☐ Greeter Ministry
☐ Worship Ministry
☐ Technical Ministry
☐ Usher Ministry

Comments, Requests or Prayer Needs

☐ For Prayer Team ☐ Confidential

_____

_____

_____

_____

_____

_____

_____

_____

_____

_____

_____

_____

_____

CHAPTER 12

Developing the Worship Experience

Purpose driven churches intentionally create purpose driven worship experiences. We have learned from Saddleback Church to look at our worship experiences through the eyes of those we are trying to reach for Christ—the unchurched. Great detail must be given to creating the worship experience that challenges believers while simultaneously speaking the language of the unchurched in this generation.

Seeker-sensitive worship is a phrase that has been talked about through the years, but how does one define seeker-sensitive worship? The phrase has become outdated and overused today. It has also come under attack as being shallow and catering to lost people instead of teaching truth to believers. Rick Muchow writes "It is a common myth that the seeker-sensitive worship service is a shallow worship service. The premise of this myth is that deep life-change and God-honoring worship must somehow be insensitive to the seeker."[1]

Dream	Design	Launch	Development	Strategic Leadership
0–3 Months	4–6 Months	6–8 Months	8–12 Months	1 Year and Beyond

How do you reach a lost person and a mature believer in the same service with the same message? Is that even possible? Absolutely! Both have the same needs, don't they? They both are dealing with the stress of balancing work and family. Both are trying to figure out how to handle their finances and deal with debt. They both have to know how to handle relationships every day of their lives. Both struggle with their dating lives or marriage challenges. They are both people, dealing with "people stuff." God's Word has their answers. The question becomes how to create a worship experience with both in mind?

Andy Stanley, Senior Pastor of North Point Community Church in Atlanta, has a great definition for reaching people in their worship services. At John Maxwell's *Catalyst Conference* he defined weekends at North Point as "a family who is expecting guests."[2] Your values do not change, what you believe does not change, but how you talk does change. Andy relates how your kids act when guests come over. Have you noticed how your kids say the most inappropriate things when guests come in the house? And, you whisper, "Shh, shh, don't say that." And, they're shouting, "Why not? I say it every day. Why not now?"

"Because we have guests. That's why."

It is the same thing in weekend worship—we are a family expecting guests. Seeker-sensitive worship is about changing the presentation and the language, not about changing theology and values. It is about food presentation. It is not about the food itself.

As you are creating a worship experience, think about how you are presenting the food. The pastor is the one who crafts the worship experience for the people. You can create a worship experience that is sensitive to people who are both inside and outside the kingdom. It takes much planning and preparation. It is hard work. Why bother? Why create a worship experience for lost people to feel comfortable? Because eternity hangs in the balance every weekend for someone in a purpose driven church.

We create worship experiences throughout the year to fulfill all five of the purposes, but we must be careful to create them through the perspective of who you are trying to reach. Rick Muchow writes, "The target does not determine the purpose. That would be target driven, not purpose driven; however it is important to look at the event from the target's perspective."[3] While creating a purpose driven worship service we must have a heart for the lost.

Be a Search-and-Rescue Church

Imagine the scene if two small children got lost in a national forest. As nightfall comes and there was still no sign of them, the police would be out in large numbers along with many people from the community. Let's say, after watching the news of the lost children on television from the comfort of your own home, you become emotionally moved to go out to the forest to help find them. What would you feel if, as you walked up on the rescue crews after nightfall, you heard laughter and singing? And as you moved closer you realized everyone was around a campfire grilling steaks and enjoying the evening under a full moon. But no one was in the forest looking for the lost children! This is a vivid description of many churches today. People are enjoying time together, gathering every weekend to sing and be fed. We tend to forget as Christ-followers we are called to be a search-and-rescue team for those who are lost.

Likewise, the mission of Jesus Christ was to seek and save the lost. Jesus was on a search-and-rescue mission—and he still is. Luke 19:10 (NIV) says, *"For the Son of Man came to seek and to save what was lost."* That is his mission statement. If we are Christ-followers, then that is our mission statement too.

Be Sensitive Toward Guests

Be sensitive to visitors. Do not do the secret handshake and other spiritual stuff. Don't talk in code, because often what we consider ritual is confusing to our guests. Be sensitive—because they may not have a clue what you are doing. Some churches have their own rituals, depending on denomination and background. Everybody in the "club" knows what to do, but outsiders do not. An unchurched guest is reminded again, "You're an outsider." When I attend some churches, I feel like an outsider. My grandmother's funeral was held in a Catholic Church in New York. I walked in and sat there, and I did not have a clue what to do. I had attended the Catholic Church as a little boy, but it had been a long time ago.

The priest knew I was a pastor and allowed me to share about my grandmother during the funeral service. I shared about her impact on my life, and then I sat down. It came time to take communion. It had been so long so I sat there uncertain of what to do. I know how we do it at The Springs, but I did not know who was to start and where to go. Do I sit here? Do they come to me? Do I go to them? Unfortunately, I was on the aisle in the front pew. Everyone was waiting for me to make a move. I sat there for what seemed like an eternity as I wrestled with whether I should move or not. I could feel the eyes of every person in the room watching me, including the priest. Finally, I decided to step out and walk to the front to receive communion. I stood in front of the priest. I could tell by his eyes I had made the wrong choice. He graciously apologized for not being able to give me communion. I was not Catholic, so I was not allowed to have communion in the Catholic Church. I was an outsider.

Give Them a Reason to Stay

The lost are looking for a reason to leave, not a reason to stay. When they visit the church, our job is to create an environment that removes barriers. Everything we do must result in taking down those barriers to belief, and making them comfortable enough to listen to truth for their lives to lead them into a relationship with Christ. After we have removed the barriers, we must build bridges into their lives.

Let me remind you that it is not about us. We must be willing to lay down our desires and wants for the lost. We must surrender ourselves to meet their needs in a way they can comprehend. Rick Warren reminds us in *The Purpose Driven Church*, "It takes unselfish mature believers to offer a seeker sensitive service."[4] The natural propensity for any church is to turn inward if we do not stoke the fires of evangelism regularly. First, take your eyes off yourself and look at others. The joy of a church start is that it can begin with a vision that promotes unselfish living, unselfish serving, and unselfish ministry. Matthew 20:28 (NIV) says, *"Just as the Son of Man did not come to be served, but to serve, and to give his life as a ransom for many."*

As the church grows, we must continue to draw a laser light focus on people far from God. Without continual refocusing, we will defuse the power of our church.

Make It a Celebration!

More than anything, people remember how the service begins and ends. As people leave the service, send them out celebrating how good God is in their lives. We always leave the worship service with a fast, upbeat song. Let them leave with a song that will stay with them through the week. We get response cards from people that say, "I feel good when I leave here." Wonderful! That is exactly how we want them to feel. Too many people think church is about getting a good spiritual spanking. The world spanks them enough. Give people something to celebrate as they reflect on the goodness of God.

Years ago I heard about a pastor who was visiting a church at Christmas. The church wanted him to become their pastor. He walked into a Wednesday-night service and there was a small group of people huddled up in a dark auditorium singing sad songs. After the service, he went Christmas shopping. As he walked by a jewelry store, he heard music and laughter pouring out onto the street. It drew him into the store; and when he entered, people shouted, "Merry Christmas!" They were *celebrating* Christmas together. He said he would have joined that jewelry store before he ever joined that church! A lot of churches have forgotten how to celebrate. Do not be one of them.

Work on Your Transitions

The flow of a service is the difference between an average service and an outstanding one. Transitions are the thread that weaves the service together, creating a seamless experience for those attending. I write out transition statements on my copy of the worship guide between segments of the service. I read each segue in order to keep the service tied together.

The comment we hear repeatedly is "The service is well thought out. Everything flows together." The whole environment we have created, in fact, is meticulously planned. Planning allows us to clearly present the message with a steady flow of elements building to a life-changing truth in the service. Keep in mind, people are accustomed to quality presentations in society that are carefully planned and executed.

Prayer is a great segue. We often pray our way into or out of worship songs. It is natural to express our heart to God during this time in the service. I am not talking about "catch up on your quiet time" prayers. One- or two-sentence prayers that connect the song to the next part of the service will do.

Announcements are not a great segue. Some churches I have visited through the years make announcements in the middle of the service. There is no connection to anything else going on. The music will stop and a guy sitting in a red velvet chair, about as far away from the podium as possible, will stand up and slowly walk to the front—accompanied by dead silence. It seems like it takes about five minutes. Any flow established in the service is gone. Concentrate on segueing each element of the service and continue working on the pace and flow of the service.

Learn to Plan as a Team

Planning as a team is a paradigm shift for most pastors. But utilizing this one point could change worship services across the country. In the established church model, worship planning, at its best, involved two people—the pastor and the worship pastor. In the majority of the older models I have observed, planning for worship was minimal. It usually involved the pastor telling the worship pastor what the sermon was going to be about for the weekend. Then the worship pastor might select songs accordingly. Each had their allotted time in the service, and if the message and music worked together, it was a work of God Almighty, because each was just responsible for his own particular segment of the service.

Purpose driven churches are a perfect place to incorporate team planning. It should take a team to create a worship experience for this generation. The team could consist of the Pastor, Worship Pastor, Program Director, Sound Team, Video Team, Drama Team, Lighting Team, Staging and Props Team. In a team effort, each element affects the others, and all are responsible for getting the life changing message across to the people. In a new church, this team will be comprised mainly of volunteers in your church from the launch team. As a church grows, these will become staff positions.

Taking the team effort one step further involves message preparation as a team. Solo preaching has become a creativity bottleneck in the local church. One person can only be creative for so long before they stagnate. Creativity and planning happen best in numbers.

We need to shatter the archaic image that the pastor goes into his study and gets the only word from God for the people. His personal study is definitely an important piece of message preparation but not the entire process. Begin to plan message series with a team of people, and tap the creativity of the people God has put around you.

We need to shatter the archaic image that the pastor goes into his study and gets the only word from God for the people.

During a church start, use the lay people God sends to brainstorm with, or work with other area church starters. Begin to build a network of other church starts in your region of the country. Visit them, have lunch with them, and learn from each other. Use your network to plan worship together.

In his *Creative Church Conference*, Ed Young says, "Team creativity alleviates speaker stress."[5] It takes the pressure off the pastor being the only one who has to develop something to teach. Secondly, it multiplies the talent base and allows people in your church and on your launch team who have creative gifts to use those gifts to advance the kingdom. This process will also help to develop other communicators.

The greatest challenge for me in the first year of The Springs was who else could teach. Everyone needs a weekend off once in a while. One way to solve this problem is to mentor someone. My brother-in-law, Phil Wilson, just started a church in the Nashville area and brought in a pastor who had helped start another church. To help this man understand Phil's philosophy and preaching style for the church, Phil had this man watch the DVD of Rick Warren's conference, *Preaching for Life Change*, and then watch other communicators who were purpose driven preachers. Now, Phil can be gone and he has another teacher.

If you are mentoring another teacher along the way, you will have someone to fill in for you when you are out of town.

Learn to tap into the power of the team that God places around you, and you will never be the same. You will communicate better than you ever have.

How to Conduct a Creative Worship Planning Meeting

Creative Worship Planning is a new concept, but one that I would strongly encourage new churches to develop. It can be challenging because it makes the pastor vulnerable to a team of people in the preparation process.

Invite creative people

That sounds obvious, but there are many people who are not creative. As you meet, you will find out who is creative and who is not. Be sure to invite people to *a meeting* and *do not* ask them to be on a team. If you discover in the meeting process they are not creative or do not have the right chemistry with the rest of the team, then thank them for coming and do not invite them back. However, if you ask them to be on a team and discover they do not fit, you are in trouble. It is easier not to invite them to another meeting than to remove them from a team.

For the team, find people who are music lovers, movie or video buffs, drama people or research librarians to help enhance your message through their areas of expertise. You will need a wide assortment of abilities, and it may take a while to build a core creative team you feel comfortable with as a leader. Remember the natural process of anything different; change, pain, growth. Team planning will cause you to grow as a leader, and as a result, cause growth in the church. After you have settled into a core creative team, continue to invite others to various meetings. This method will keep the avenues open to discover new team members.

Create a feedback mentality

It has been said that feedback is the breakfast of champions. Hal Mayer, our Executive Pastor, brought feedback to The Springs. After one of his first weekends at the church, he met me after the first service and asked if I wanted any feedback on my message. My initial thought was, *was the message that bad?* Hal sat down with me and walked through all the points of the message, giving me constructive feedback. It was constructive because it built a better message for the next two services in the weekend. That is what feedback is supposed to do, make us better communicators. Today, I still look forward to meeting with the feedback team immediately following the first service.

In a creative meeting, the leader must set the tone for feedback. Ask for feedback on the last service, and do not get defensive. Thank those who give feedback, and compliment them on their insight. Always encourage them to use feedback as a ladder not a hammer. What can we do differently, how can we improve? Remember the parts that went well and refine the points that did not work. Feedback should bring fresh ideas not simply correction. With the feedback process in place, your team will improve every week.

Plan in series

Planning in a message series format takes creative pressure off of a team. Separate weekly "stand-alone" messages, in contrast to a series, are more labor intensive. There are so many great resources for message series ideas: *Pastors.com*, *CreativePastors.com*, *Willowcreek.com*, and *Northpoint.org*, just to mention a few. Prayerfully select some series that will meet the needs of your congregation.

If you are planning an original series, brainstorm a relevant title. Titles are extremely important in the promotion and development of the series. Remember there are no bad ideas. If people immediately shoot down ideas it will stifle the creative process. Every idea is a good idea. Listen and let the team talk through it in an atmosphere of acceptance. Remember that this meeting is designed for dreaming, not doubting. Nothing is impossible. This is a dreaming session not a problem-solving session. If you lapse into attempting to resolve how to accomplish every idea, you will lose creativity.

Once the big idea for a series has been selected, begin to break it down into four to six different messages. We have found that after six weeks, a series tends to get old for our team and the church. Four weeks is the typical length of a series at The Springs, because it keeps the congregation's attention and keeps them wondering what is next. After the series has been selected, the weekly creative team meetings can focus on crafting the individual services for the series.

Come prepared

Set up a room with everything necessary. Creative meetings are for brainstorming. Work in a room with a white board or use giant Post-it® notes to stick on the walls. Designate someone on the team as the note taker, responsible for compiling all the ideas from the meeting and e-mailing them to the team. Stock the room with snacks and drinks. Food fuels creativity! (I believe that is a scientific fact, or maybe just wishful thinking.)

Come prepared to spark creativity within the team. As the leader, you should come with some series ideas and creative elements you have already researched. This legwork will get the creative juices flowing in the meeting. We have had creative meetings that were duds because I was not prepared to lead. Bring titles and big ideas for the series or message, and some foundational Scripture. Share what God is working in your heart about the series.

We have learned to break the meeting into two parts. The first part is a thirty-minute meeting to introduce the series and message titles. With that information, the team can show up for the next meeting ready to be creative with possible resources and music. When the entire team has a chance to research before the meeting, it makes for a highly productive meeting. Without good preparation, there tends to be a lot of awkward silence in the meeting. If a meeting goes flat creatively, call it quits and schedule another time to meet.

If possible, schedule the meeting in the morning hours when people are fresh. If mornings are not possible, select a time when people are not overly tired. Creativity tends to break down when people are tired and hungry. Have we discussed the importance of food at these meetings?

Limit meetings to a two-hour maximum. After two hours, creativity tends to stagnate and people get tired, so provide breaks for your team.

Weave in creative elements

Once you have begun working on individual messages, introduce creative elements into the worship service. Creative elements can be video clips, message video roll-ins, dramas, testimonies, interviews, dance, or a powerful performance song. A list of sources for these elements can be found in the Appendix. Vary the types of elements throughout the series to keep the service from becoming too predictable.

The God moments

Search for the "God moment" in each worship service. It may be a point in the message with a particular story, it may be a testimony, it may be a drama, song, or video clip. Every service can have a

Every service can have a "moment" where it captures the hearts of the people.

"moment" where it captures the hearts of the people. Even with all the planning, sometimes the God moment may surprise you. We have planned many services when we thought one creative element would be the moment, and that was the very part of the service that fell flat.

In all your planning as a team, always remember that eternity hangs in the balance for people in every service. As a purpose driven church, you have now created an environment which partners with the Holy Spirit as he changes lives and eternities. Stand in awe of God as he uses your team to provide God encounters that cause people to cross the line of faith. What an incredible privilege. Go team!

---

[1] Muchow, Rick, "Implementing PD: Programming on Purpose," 2006, **www.purposedriven.com**, http://www.purposedriven.com/en-US/WorshipCommunity/ImplementingPD/implementingpdmarch.htm

[2] Stanley, Andy, Catalyst Conference (Alpharetta, Ga., 2003).

[3] Muchow, "Implementing PD: Programming on Purpose"

[4] Warren, *The Purpose Driven Church*, (Grand Rapids, Mich.: Zondervan, 1995), 250.

[5] Young, Ed, C3 Conference, (Dallas, Tex.), 2004.

CHAPTER 13

Installing the Purpose Driven CLASS System

Earlier in the book, I mentioned that God had given The Springs a train, and Purpose Driven was the track to ride on to grow the church. The simplicity of the track is found in the CLASS System. CLASS stands for Christian Life and Service Seminars. The four classes are the foundation of the Purpose Driven system which needs to be imbedded in your new church; and they are the markers for the spiritual growth and development of people in your congregation. CLASS offers a simple, reproducible model for tracking spiritual growth points in the church. Notice I wrote "spiritual growth points" and not "spiritual growth." The classes are points of potential spiritual growth, but, just because someone attends a class does not mean they are growing spiritually. Information exchanged in class does not equal maturity; acting on what one learns brings about maturity.

Dream	Design	Launch	Development	Strategic Leadership
0–3 Months	4–6 Months	6–8 Months	8–12 Months	1 Year and Beyond

Each class is intended to take a person deeper into levels of commitment in the local church. At the conclusion of each class, the attendee is asked to sign a covenant to act on what they have learned. Saddleback Church offers their classes on *www.Pastors.com* for purchase. The church planter can purchase the audio version, the written transcript and notes, as well as the PowerPoint® for the class presentation.

- **CLASS 101—Introduction to Our Church Family**

    101 teaches the topics of salvation, baptism, and communion, along with the purposes, targets, structure, and affiliations of the church.

- **CLASS 201—Introduction to Spiritual Maturity**

    201 focuses on the four basic habits every Christian needs to grow to spiritual maturity: Time in God's Word, prayer, tithing, and fellowship.

- **CLASS 301—Discovering My S.H.A.P.E. for Ministry**

    301 teaches through the S.H.A.P.E. process, learning how God can use your Spiritual gifts, Heart, Abilities, Personality and life Experience to minister to others in need.

- **CLASS 401—Discovering My Life Mission**

    401 focuses on equipping and empowering your core for world and life-changing missions while teaching them how to share their faith.

People need to see a track for spiritual growth in their lives, and CLASS offers that track. The baseball diamond on page 155 is a visual of running the bases toward living a purpose driven life. Once a person completes the classes, they have the information to live a balanced life focusing on God's purposes for them. The synergy that is created when an entire church focuses on God's purposes is powerful in the life of the church.

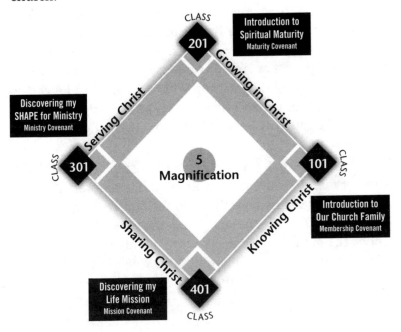

CLASS 101—Membership Class

It is essential that people commit to membership in the church. This is the ownership module for growing Christ followers. People become what they are committed to in life. If they never commit to the local church, they will inevitably flounder in spiritual growth. They must tether their lives to a community of Christ-followers found in the local church.

The core elements of a successful CLASS 101 are:

(1) Purposes of the Church

(2) Core Values

(3) Core Beliefs

(4) Strategy

(5) Membership Covenant

It is best to start with Saddleback's version and over time adapt it to your own church's distinctives. Saddleback's CLASS 101 is a four-hour course, while at The Springs we have adjusted it to a two-and-a-half hour class. One of the keys to a successful CLASS 101 in a new church is that the lead pastor must teach the class. The Springs was eight-years old before I gave away some of the teaching responsibilities in CLASS 101. The church needs to hear the vision from the visionary leader. Do not delegate this responsibility for at least five years into the church.

As a new church starts, there is an unseen centrifugal pull to offer membership quickly. Resist the urge to offer CLASS 101 until at least two months into the church launch. In the first months of a new church, everyone is still trying to learn about the church. Give people time to adjust to the weekly services before offering membership. Your launch team will bring the most pressure to join the church. A desire to join the church is healthy and understandable; capitalize on that desire by allowing a healthy anticipation and excitement for membership to build.

Two to three months into the beginning of weekly services roll out the idea of CLASS 101 through a vision weekend. Teach about the vision of your church, and begin sign-ups for your first CLASS 101 three weeks before the class event—not sooner. If the promotion is done well, most of the people who are attending will come to CLASS 101. There should be a buzz throughout the church as you offer "the first membership CLASS 101."

The frequency of CLASS 101 will be dictated by the growth of the church and the flow of first time guests. After the initial class, allow at least two to three months before offering another one. During the first year of the church, you should offer CLASS 101 no more than three or four times. Remember the importance of having a critical mass in each class. There is nothing worse than having a membership class with only four people in attendance. Low membership class attendance sends a bad signal about the health and future of the church. "Critical mass" is subjective. In the early days of The Springs, we wanted at least twenty people to attend each CLASS 101. If our registrations were below that, we canceled the class and rescheduled.

Realize that there is a deficit between sign-ups and attendance in classes. Typically 60–75% of the people who sign up will actually show up. To increase your show up rate, never promote the class more than three weeks out from the date. After people have signed up, follow up with a confirmation phone call the week of the class.

Remember to offer childcare for all classes. Remove as many obstacles to attendance as possible. Do not divide CLASS 101 over multiple weeks. This is usually a recipe for disaster. People are more willing to commit to one time block rather than multiple dates. If the class is divided up, you then have to schedule make up classes for each section, and administration becomes a nightmare. What if someone, for example, misses the section on salvation, but they want to join the church?

Classes should be offered in a single time block. The best time and day for the class will be dictated by your own community culture. We have found what many purpose driven churches have found, that Sunday afternoon at 4:00 p.m. works for highest attendance in our classes. We have experimented with Saturday morning time slots and Wednesday evening schedules, but we always come back to Sunday late afternoon times.

Putting two to three months between classes also sets the classes apart as a special event. As the church grows and gets older, you will learn the rhythm of membership. For us at The Springs, we offer CLASS 101 every six weeks. This allows us to expect a class of between 40 to 100 people every six weeks.

Once you have offered your first CLASS 101, recruit table hosts for the next classes. Table hosts are church members who are leaders in your church. Train the hosts to build relationships with new members, inviting them into small groups or ministries. In our CLASS 101, our table hosts are usually small group leaders who strategically invite people into their groups. Each class should be used to lead people into next steps toward maturity in Christ. Remember maturity is not just what you know, it is what you do.

CLASS 201—Spiritual Maturity Class

Once you have spent the first year offering CLASS 101, it is time to introduce CLASS 201. This is the maturity class that focuses on the habits of a Christ-follower. Remember to focus the first year on building a crowd and assimilating them into membership through CLASS 101. Your propensity and the cry of some people will be to "take me deeper." You may *want* to begin small groups and develop believers, but move slowly. It takes time to build a healthy church. Resist the urge to offer all the classes too quickly.

Remember, purpose driven churches are built from the outside in. Build commitment one circle at a time. The first circle is building the crowd, and then assimilating them into the congregation. In the first year, remember that people are looking for relationships and responsibilities. You can offer both of those through CLASS 101 and ministry opportunities. One of our core values is "Every Member is a Minister." We have found that most people who want to join also have a desire to get involved in ministry. Therefore we move people into ministry as soon as possible by offering ministry sign ups at the conclusion of CLASS 101.

Introduce CLASS 201 with a church wide message series on spiritual growth. Since CLASS 201 teaches about prayer, tithing, and time with God, build a series that addresses one of those topics wrapped in a felt need of the people. If you are going to teach about tithing, wrap it in the felt need of getting out of debt. If you are going to teach about small groups, wrap it in the felt need of loneliness or desire for friendship. This type of series will give you the opportunity to teach sections of CLASS 201 in the weekend messages, and allow for an abbreviated CLASS 201.

The first CLASS 201 should be primarily taught by the lead pastor, as is the case when first introducing all of the classes. After the first installment of CLASS 201, you can pass the class to a qualified teacher. Using your best teachers allows them to develop the class and improve their presentations, while giving them ownership in the Purpose Driven Model.

If you have not already done so, CLASS 201 will be a great time to launch small groups in your church. This class should be a great catalyst for spiritual growth in a young church and will begin a year of spiritual maturity, balancing the crowd, the congregation, and now the committed.

CLASS 301—Ministry Class

By the middle to end of the second year, CLASS 301 can be introduced. CLASS 301 will help people discover their S.H.A.P.E. for ministry. Through the S.H.A.P.E. process, people will learn how God can use their spiritual gifts, heart, abilities, personality and life experience to minister to others in need. This process will allow the church to put the right people in the right places of ministry, instead of simply filling slots.

Most people will already be involved in a ministry before they get to CLASS 301. The class will give them the foundation to fully understand ministry in the local church, and it may give them the freedom to test drive or begin a new ministry opportunity.

When you first make CLASS 301 available, you can launch it through a message series on ministry. Once again, use the same format as introducing CLASS 201 to teach sections of the class in your messages, and offer a first time abbreviated

CLASS 301. To punctuate the power of ministry in your church, host a Ministry Fair the weekend following CLASS 301. This weekend will be used to introduce all the ministries in your church, and to recruit new people for them. People are always surprised to see all the different ministry opportunities that are available, and the number of people who work behind the scenes to make the church happen.

CLASS 401—Evangelism and Missions Class

Approximately six months after introducing CLASS 301, it is time to roll out the final class in the CLASS System—CLASS 401. CLASS 401 will move people back out into the community and the world through evangelism. By the end of the third year of a new church, the entire CLASS System should be in place.

CLASS 401 is dedicated to helping your members discover and realize their place in the world and in their own communities. This class has three primary emphases:

(1) Learning to Share My Faith
(2) Becoming a "World-Class" Christian
(3) Discovering God's Mission for My Life

CLASS 401 will dovetail into the P.E.A.C.E. Plan Rick Warren is introducing to the Christian Community. P.E.A.C.E. is the strategy to attack the five giants of the world:

(1) Spiritual Darkness
(2) Lack of servant leaders around the world
(3) Poverty
(4) Disease
(5) Ignorance

Each of these giants will be toppled through the efforts of mobilizing the Christian community for global P.E.A.C.E.:

Planting churches
Equipping servant-leaders

Assisting the poor
Caring for the sick
Educating the next generation

Once your church has introduced the entire CLASS system, be prepared to enter the P.E.A.C.E. Plan to reach the world for Christ.

As you start implementing the CLASS system, realize that there is an attrition rate from CLASS 101 to CLASS 401. Unfortunately, everyone who attends 101 will not make it through to CLASS 401. This truth is represented visually through the circles of commitment.

The congregation is smaller than the crowd, the committed is smaller than the congregation, and the core is smaller than the committed. Our task is to continually and strategically attempt to lead our people to take next steps toward a deeper commitment to Christ.

CHAPTER 14

First-Year Ministries

Student ministry was my life and calling for ten years. I never wanted to leave it, and I told God and others I did not *ever* want to be a senior pastor. Leading vibrant student ministries was what I did best. One of my personal struggles during the first year at The Springs was not offering a quality program for our students. My temptation was to start a student ministry and lead both it and the church. I had always served in larger churches with big budgets and multiple staff to meet the needs of thousands of people, but as a new church, there was no money, staff, or facilities. I had to come to the harsh reality that for us, student ministry was not a first-year ministry. Instead, we chose to offer a volunteer-led youth ministry that was more like a large small group.

One challenge in the first year of a new church is to determine which ministries should start more quickly than others. Because the first year of a church is about the weekends, every ministry must enhance the weekend experience. If a ministry does not

Dream	Design	Launch	Development	Strategic Leadership
0–3 Months	4–6 Months	6–8 Months	8–12 Months	1 Year and Beyond

enhance the weekends, leave it alone until the weekends are solid. Andy Stanley, in *The Next Generation Leader*, writes that a leader must "only do what only you can do."[1] His challenge is for leaders to do less to accomplish more. The same holds true for a new church. Be content in the first year with doing less extraneous ministries to accomplish more eternal impact on the weekend. If, for example, your resources, both people and finances, are scattered across multiple ministries, many average things will get done, instead of exceptional things. Most people far from God will not come back to an average weekend service. People will not continue inviting their friends to an average church. Since the weekend service *is* the church to guests, make it the best presentation of Christ possible or guests may not stay long enough to see what other ministries are offered. Choose now to invest your resources and heart into the weekends during the first year. Sell your core team on the value of the weekend ministries.

Basic first-year ministries will include: Worship Team, Greeters, Ushers, Children's Ministry, and Small Groups. All of these, with the exception of Small Groups, must be in place by the time a church launches, and then built stronger throughout the first year. In the launch process, these ministries will be skeletal frameworks of future ministries. Over the course of the year, you must begin to put skin and muscle on them. This chapter will lead you through that process.

Music Ministry

Building a worship team from scratch

If you do not have a worship leader, you do not have a worship service . . .

If you do not have a worship leader, you do not have a worship service—you have a small group. Worship through music is essential for the weekend service. Finding a worship leader, however, can be a daunting task for a new church. Often times, we make the search more unrealistic by placing our assumptions on the position. We assume we need a full-time worship pastor. We assume we cannot afford someone of great quality. Place your assumptions aside, and allow God to provide. Remember God has already tapped someone to lead worship for the church, you just have to find them. Let me share some of the first-year lessons from my journey in building a worship team.

Hire a worship leader before a worship pastor

Hire somebody who can be a part-time worship leader before you run out and hire a full-time worship pastor. When Teddi and I were called to start The Springs, we did not know where to turn for a worship leader, so I called my friend, Jeff Scott. Jeff worked with me in student ministry in Ocala but had moved to Atlanta. He would have been the perfect person to lead worship for us if he had not relocated, because he played keyboards, wrote music, and was a gifted vocalist. I told Jeff that God had called us to start a new church in Ocala, and asked him to pray for us as we started. Jeff's reaction was classic—he laughed. Jeff knew me and thought I was crazy to leave the student ministry I loved, but he told me he would pray for us.

Then, to his surprise and mine, Jeff called me back the next day and said, "I don't know what it's about, but I'm supposed to be a part of it. If you can get me to Ocala, I'll lead worship for free."

And so, for a grand total of $99 a week for airfare, Jeff flew in on Saturdays and flew home on Sundays every week for an entire year just to lead worship at The Springs. Of course, God has blessed my friend many times since then because of his heart for ministry.

Do not limit your search for a worship leader to your city. The world has become a smaller place through air travel. In addition, there are many college students who would be excellent worship leaders for a new church. Before you launch, do the research and discover a part-time worship leader. Look around, and find somebody that can serve temporarily.

By the time Jeff had finished at The Springs, he had built a worship team and there was someone from that team who took up the leadership mantel for the next season. We were two-years old when we hired Derrick Shirley, our first full-time worship pastor.

Stay actively involved in the music ministry

Staying involved in the music ministry is not a control issue, it is a formation issue. Since the pastor determines the worship style, he has to be involved in the guidance of the song selection in the formative days of a church start. Although I knew very little about music, I knew a lot about who we were trying to reach.

Do not surrender complete leadership of the music ministry to someone you "think" understands the vision for the church. In the first year of a new church, the pastor has to keep an eye on the pulse of all the elements of the church—especially the worship service. With the growth after the first year, it is impossible to monitor things as closely. That is one of the benefits of the early days of a church start. Spend the first year building a solid foundation of leadership in your music ministry while you have the time and ability to be intricately involved. As the church grows, you will not have this luxury.

Determine your position on paid musicians

At The Springs we did not pay any musicians who were on the stage, because everybody on the stage was a volunteer. Many churches today pay all their musicians. Others see the music ministry as an outreach tool where musicians are allowed to play on their worship team as the church builds relationships with them to lead them to faith in Christ. We have found it essential to determine your position on musicians early. Neither position is wrong, but they are different.

Using volunteers is a challenge, but the team unity and camaraderie are powerful. And as the church grows, you will see that musicians attract musicians. Musicians are like the rest of us, they want to be in a place where there are people like them. If you happen to draw professional musicians you will tap into an artery of other musicians. In many cities, the only venue for musicians is in the local club scene. Musicians are drawn to life, sound, and other musicians. When a church comes along that uses today's music and instruments, there will come a flow of musicians to that church. There is a connection among musicians that brings harmony to a team, as each one finds their place.

Protect the stage

Protect the integrity of the stage. People perceive those on the stage to be leaders, even when they are not. So be careful about who is allowed on the stage. Several times we made the mistake of letting someone get up and play or sing before we knew them well enough. One man was a talented musician, writer, and singer. After I had delivered my message, he sang a song he had written in response to the teaching. It was an incredible song. We thought we had hit pay dirt, until one of our members came up after the service. He was a prosecuting attorney for the city and recognized the man as someone who was in the court system with some pretty serious charges against him. When we confronted the man that week, he became angry and defensive and never returned.

Know the people that walk up on the stage. Have a process for them—a process so you can actually sit down with them and find out who they are.

Learn contentment

The challenge with modeling yourself after some of the great churches today is that many have had ten to fifteen years to build their worship teams. No church start is going to be Saddleback Church in the first few years. However, you can be better than they were when they started. Most great churches struggle to build quality music ministries. Remember it takes time to build a quality worship team which has musical talent and depth. Learn to be content with God's provision of people. Love and develop the people God sends. He did not call you to be any other church. He called you to be you in your community and reach your generation there. At each level of musical quality, we were content to develop the talent God had sent us. We learned to do the best we could with what we had. $- - - \blacktriangleright$

Redefine the word "excellence"

Excellence is doing the best we can with what we have.

$\blacktriangleleft - - -$

The Springs has always desired to honor God with excellence, but there is a dark side to excellence. It is perfectionism, and the problem with perfectionism is that perfection can never be achieved. So we redefined excellence. Excellence is doing the best we can with what we have. Therefore, the definition of excellence changes as a church grows. The more you have, the more you can do. There is nothing wrong with wanting to be the best you can be, but there is something seriously wrong with trying to be perfect.

One of the first services at The Springs was held downstairs in an office complex, sitting at desks. In 1994, Jared, our nine-year old, was flipping transparencies with song lyrics. By today's standard, that was a terrible service. We used a video clip from a movie and had a short dramatic presentation. With about forty people in attendance, I rented a video projector for a three-minute video clip. We did the best we could with what we had, and gave those forty people the best worship experience we could in a downstairs office complex full of desks.

Ask yourself, is our vocalist doing the best he or she can? Is our guitarist doing the best possible job? We have had musicians through the years who continued to develop their talent. We have also had musicians who did not desire to raise the level of their talent through practice. As a church grows and a worship team develops, the quality of music should improve. Because of our definition of excellence, excellence became an escalating value. Simply put, people who sang on our worship team when we were six-months old possibly would not make the team when we are eleven-years old. Someone who ran lights when we had one tree of lights might not run lights when we have fourteen computerized lights. Obviously, the quality rises as the team develops.

Once, we lost our keyboardist and had to worship to cassettes. We quickly found a MIDI player could be utilized instead. Another time, we had six vocalists and a keyboard player. We wanted to show our people what the vision of a full band looked like. So, as we were singing "Ancient of Days," we faded up a video of Ron Kenoly leading a huge band and thousands of worshipers. It was a risk. We did not know if the people would interact with the video or not. They loved it. They locked in. They were clapping and going with the video. No one was more shocked than I was. Obviously, we could not do that every week, but it worked on several occasions.

Use the equipment and resources available to you in each season of ministry. We have used cassettes, CDs, MIDI players and videos. Keep growing and advancing in the quality of equipment and instrumentalists. Be content and faithful in the little things, and God will give you greater things!

Develop your service

Learn contentment, but do not get comfortable. Keep growing and developing your worship experience. The theme of one presidential election was "It's the economy, stupid." As a church start, we had to remember, "It's the service, stupid." For a young church, everything rides on that weekend experience. Do not scatter resources among all the other programs and activities people want you to start. Stay focused on enhancing the worship service. Everything else in the church flows out of worship. People will forgive you for not having top-notch small group or adult Sunday school ministries, but they will not forgive you for a boring worship service. Of course, they will not tell you that either, they simply will not come back.

Children's Ministry

When we began The Springs, I underestimated the power of a dynamic children's ministry. We made a serious strategic error in our weekends regarding children. We only offered childcare for preschool and nothing for older children. Through some very painful experiences, I have learned that a dynamic children's ministry is essential to a new church. Dozens of families came to visit us the first year, and after seeing that we offered nothing for their children during the worship service, they simply walked out. They did not even stay for the service. Unchurched parents today do not want to sit through a service with a squirming, talking child who is bored. To capture families, you must offer a full children's ministry at the same time as your adult worship service.

Teddi began our children's ministry. It was not her passion, but she saw the need and stepped in to meet it. She poured her life into our children's ministry, and developed leaders with a passion for those kids. The ministry grew so quickly that we soon needed to hire a full-time children's minister. Teddi did what she has done many times through the years, and that is to get a ministry growing, develop leaders, and pass it on to them.

Develop a children's ministry staff out of your launch team. Cast a vision to them about the importance of training up the next generation. Take them to a conference or to a thriving purpose driven church to catch the vision, and then invest in resources they need to make it happen. Resources for children's ministry today are easily available. There is a new generation of churches who are developing and producing children's ministry material for other churches. Saddleback has *ALL STARS*, built around the five purposes, and a children's ministry conference. Willow Creek offers *Promiseland Curriculum* for children, and has been the front-runner in children's ministry conferences. Fellowship Church is offering *G-Force Curriculum* and a children's ministry conference. North Point Community Church has *Kidstuf*. All of the resources have the ability to assist a new church in fast-tracking a quality children's ministry. Some children's curriculum is video-based, such as *Kidmo*. See the resource list in the back for various sites and materials. Though each has its unique fingerprint, they all have common elements to a quality children's ministry.

Fun must be a core value for any children's ministry. Our society is very entertainment driven as evidenced by the way we go to the movies, watch TV, play video games, and spend thousands of dollars to take trips to theme parks. If you can put

> *Fun must be a core value for any children's ministry.*

fun in your children's ministry, then kids are going to be excited about coming back. When parents pick up their children they typically ask two questions. The first is, "Did you have fun?" The second is, "What did you learn?" In a children's ministry, we must focus on meeting those two needs for families—fun and learning.

If you invest in a quality children's ministry, it will become a magnet for families in your community. Often churches treat children as a secondary ministry rather than a primary concern. We have discovered when we pour finances into children we get parental returns. In 2001, Teddi and I visited Granger Community Church in South Bend, Indiana. We visited on the day of the grand opening of their new Children's Center. As we toured the facility, we passed the children's check-in area outside the worship center. After registering the kids in their computer system, they brought them behind the counter and put them in plastic tubes to *slide down* into their classrooms! A video monitor was mounted above each slide, allowing the parents to see them come out the bottom of the slide into a teacher's hands. Both teacher and kids waved to their parents and then went into their class. Let me ask you a question: Do you think those kids wanted to come back the next week? Do you think they had fun? Granger Community exploded with even more growth after building their Children's Center.

While a new church cannot build a facility like Granger's, you can build an environment that is fun and educational. Utilizing resources available to churches today allows children's leaders in new churches to focus on creating environments that are high-energy and kid-friendly. Kids also need an identity in their ministry. We wrestled with a name and a theme for our children's ministry and finally named it Springsville, a town for little believers to learn about Jesus. We have divided the town into age-appropriate areas. Springsville Park is the nursery, Springsville Clubhouse is for four- and five-year olds, Springsville Stadium is for K–2nd grade, and Springsville Theater is for 3rd–5th grade. Every church must build an environment kids can call their own. If you do not have enough creative energy at the start of the church, borrow someone else's name. Imitation is the best form of flattery. So go ahead and flatter someone's children's ministry.

We must also create an environment for our children that is safe. Parents must be confident when they drop their children off that they are secure. For a new church start meeting in temporary facilities, the security issue must be of the utmost importance. Not only must the children's area be secure, but the people who are working with the children must have security clearance. Pay the expense of having background checks on everyone who works with your kids. New churches can be a target for child molesters, because they could be aware that you may not have all of the security systems in place yet. For added security, have some men stand in the area as ministry guards. Parents will appreciate every extra effort you take to protect their children.

Recruiting volunteers will be a first-year challenge. Most people's past experience with children's ministry has been baby-sitting, and that is boring. Nobody wants to simply baby-sit; they want to make a difference. Pray for and search out someone who will be your children's ministry leader. Every new church needs a champion for the children. As you begin the first few months of Preview Services, borrow volunteers temporarily from sponsoring churches. After your official launch, find people to serve alternating weeks or months in children's ministry. Once volunteers are in the rotation, do everything you can to value them. Let them know they are appreciated and important in the life of a child and their family. Cast a vision for the impact of a top-notch children's ministry. They are part of a church within a church reaching the next generation. Empower them to lead and connect that generation to a God who is passionately in love with them.

One word of caution regarding volunteers: do not burn out your people. Worker stress is high in new churches. If volunteers have to work every weekend, they will burn out. Do not let individuals serve for months at a time without a break. If you over work your volunteers, the children's ministry will gain a reputation of using people up. It can take years to rebuild a children's ministry. Often a pastor's spouse is the one who takes the leadership of children. The consequence of stress and burn out if unchecked could destroy not only a ministry but a marriage, so make certain *all* of your volunteers are on a rotation in children's ministry. They need to be in adult worship to be rejuvenated and refreshed.

Children are not only the future of the church, but ministering to them can be the foundation of a new church. In a children's ministry, fun and biblical teaching are core values. Build a make-believe city for little people where they can learn believable truth. Offer kid-style worship that is alive and exciting. As you build the children's ministry you will build a large volunteer army who not only love the next generation, but love serving together as a team. Friendships will be formed as lives are transformed. Your children's ministry should be the talk of your church and your community. If it is, then kids will drag their parents to your church, because they do not want to miss church. And while the children are learning and having fun, their parents will be hearing biblical truth for their generation in an environment created just for them.

First-Impression Ministries

A new church must work diligently to create a warm welcoming weekend environment for adults as well. We have talked a lot about creating this environment, but as stated, greeters and ushers are foundational ministries in your first year. In essence, they are a tag team. Greeters are the welcoming team who get people into the service, and the ushers are protectors of the worship service. Greeting should begin in the parking lot, and carry through the lobby to the worship center; then ushers pick up at the doors. Ushers assist people in finding seats, and meet every need of people in the service. These two positions comprise the foundation of the first impression people get from your church.

The natural assumptions are that anyone can serve in these positions, and they require no training. Both assumptions are wrong. Select people from your launch team, who exude warmth and friendliness. Offer training for greeters and ushers. Equip and empower them to be the first impression of your church to a lost world.

As the church grows larger, you must intentionally grow smaller at the same time.

Small Groups

In the first few months of a new church, it often feels like a family. A smaller church has a built-in sense of belonging. As the church grows larger, you must intentionally grow smaller at the same time. The natural tendency of many church planters is to begin a new church with small groups immediately. Do not begin small groups before you are averaging about 150–200 people in worship. Growth dictates a fostering of relationships. Teddi and I realized there were a growing number of young married couples attending The Springs in the first year. They were all faithfully attending, but were not connected in relationships. We began our first small group for young married couples. I will never forget the first night we met together. As I looked around the room, we were all familiar strangers. We knew each other, but we did not really know each other. The only common ground we shared was the season of our lives. My initial thought in the awkwardness of the first meeting was, *this will never work.* Within three meetings, I could not believe the transformation of relationships. And to this day, almost ten years later, those relationships are still strong.

Teddi and I were the parents of the group, considerably older, with two children of our own. Within the year, all of the couples had children or were pregnant. When Teddi got pregnant at 37-years old, we decided we had better get out of that group! We were busy birthing a church, and had no intention of birthing our third child at the same time. God had other plans for our lives. We could not imagine our lives without Luke, our Springs baby. He is growing up at The Springs and has never known another church. We are still connected to those special friendships from our first small group, and our children play together. Small groups do what a worship service cannot—they connect hearts and lives.

While small groups are not a weekend ministry, they must develop to assimilate people from the weekend. The weekend will attract people to your church, but relationships will keep them there. We have learned a lot about small groups through the years, but have much to learn as well. Small groups are like diamonds—they are multifaceted. And I don't know if anyone ever fully captures all the power and beauty of small groups within a church. It is an ongoing journey. Every time you think you have seen it all, another miracle of relationships explodes on the scene through a small group. The reality is small groups take a lot of hard work for any size church. With 3,000 people currently attending The Springs, small groups are still hard work but worth it, for we know they are invaluable in building a community of Christ-followers.

It is easier to incorporate small groups into the DNA of a young church. Willow Creek small group ministry teaches that we are to be churches of small groups not simply churches that offer small groups. This statement is easier said than done. The biblical foundation of small groups must be taught in worship services. Jesus had a small group—his twelve disciples. In Acts, the New Testament church modeled small groups, as they met in temple courts and from house to house, both large and small groups worshiping together. Teach a message series on the power and purpose of small groups. As people leave the worship service, station pre-enlisted small group leaders outside the doors. Challenge people to act on what they have learned today by signing up for a small group. Always give them an opportunity to be doers of the Word.

Hook people into small groups with a short-term commitment. Many people are concerned about signing up for a commitment that is unending. We live in a generation of short-term commitments: parents register their kids for a season of baseball or basketball, they offer to serve on boards for one year, and in college they register by semesters. We need to allow them to see an end to their small group commitment. We have found that by offering short-term topical small groups, we attract a larger number of people to small groups. For instance, after teaching a message series on marriage, we always offer twelve-week marriage small groups. Through the sermon series, we have revealed issues in people's lives, and a small group gives them a safe place to talk about and work through those issues.

Purpose Driven Ministry's campaign, *40 Days of Purpose*, captured this same principle by offering short term Purpose Groups studying *The Purpose Driven Life* by Rick Warren. The average church participating in the campaign saw 102% growth in their number of small groups. The Springs went from around 40 groups to 120 groups during *40 Days of Purpose*.

Approximately 80% of the groups that commit to a short-term study will stay together as a group. Short-term small groups are the hook for long-term commitment. What happens is, people begin to weave their lives together in a community of believers. They have prayed together, grown together, laughed and cried together. In essence, they are doing life together. Small groups are the church at its best.

Small groups are the network of support your church will need as it grows. When people are in the hospital, their small group visits them. When people have loved ones die, their small groups care for them. When people have financial needs, their small group is the first to tend to their needs.

Often our hospital ministry has gone to visit one of our members when a tragedy has struck, only to discover a small group of people surrounding the member. When someone is in a small group at The Springs, I do not worry about them. But until someone is connected with a small group, they really are not connected to the church. Again, small groups need to begin after your first year to build a fully functioning community of Christ-followers.

---

[1] Stanley, Andy, *The Next Generation Leader: 5 Essentials for Those Who Will Shape the Future*, (Sisters, Ore.: Multnomah Publishers, Inc., 2003), 17

Stage Five

Strategic Leadership Stage

- Strategic Leadership
- Hiring Staff
- Riding Momentum

CHAPTER 15

Strategic Leadership

In *The Next Generation Leader*, Andy Stanley writes, "The more you know about leadership, the faster you grow as a leader, and the farther you are able to go as a leader."[1] Purpose driven churches require purpose driven leaders; leaders who are constantly observing and absorbing leadership lessons from others. Non-developing leaders are one of the main reasons the average church in America has less than 100 people in worship on Sunday morning. Purpose driven churches are growing churches because they have growing leaders. Growth is normal for all healthy bodies. My youngest son, Luke, is nine-years old. He is over four feet tall and weighs in at seventy-eight pounds. If three years from now he has not grown anymore, I would be very concerned. I would consult doctors and specialists to see why he was not developing as a young man. There would have to be barriers that are keeping him from growing, because healthy children grow. The same is true of the church. Barriers keep us from growing.

Dream	Design	Launch	Development	Strategic Leadership
0–3 Months	4–6 Months	6–8 Months	8–12 Months	1 Year and Beyond

Church starters must continually develop as leaders or they will become the barriers for growth in their churches. Everything rises and falls on leadership. Purpose driven leaders learn how to lead larger by continuing to grow and develop their leadership skills.

The first leadership shift takes place in *what* a pastor does on a daily basis. Howard Hendricks, a professor at Dallas Theological Seminary, has said, "The secret of concentration is elimination." A true leader learns the art of elimination. At a staff retreat, this became painfully clear when our worship pastor challenged me to stop trying to do everything I thought was part of my job description. On a whiteboard, we listed everything I was responsible for at The Springs. The list was twenty-seven items long. On another board, we made a list of what I needed to be doing, those certain things I am gifted and called to do. The list was only four items: teach, vision cast, lead the church, and pray for God's direction. I still remember him standing up in that conference room and saying, "This is easy. You have to stop doing these twenty-three other things." It was not easy. There were good things on that list, things a pastor was *supposed* to do. Weddings are no longer on my "to-do list." Counseling is not in my job description. Funerals are not performed by me anymore. These were difficult choices, but the staff was right. I had to let go to grow with The Springs.

This leadership shift has to happen as a church grows beyond 200 people. Rick Warren says that "as a church grows, two things have to happen: the pastor has to give up the ministries and the people have to give up the pastor." You can grow a church to 200–300 with ministry skills, but you grow beyond 200–300 with leadership skills.

Where do you learn leadership skills? Avail yourself of training and conferences. At least one conference a year is essential for the growing leader. Continue to develop leadership skills. The skills used to grow a church to 200 will keep it from growing beyond 200. Be willing to change and shift; an effective leader has to be reinvented every several years. Ed Young challenged me to "lead The Springs like it is twice as big as it is." Lead larger. There is more training available today on the subject of leadership than in any other generation: books, tapes, CDs, videos, conferences.

Decades ago, Frank Tillapaugh wrote a book called *Unleashing the Church*.[2] The book introduced a new paradigm in churches, mobilizing lay people to do ministry, rather than just the paid staff. We must unleash the power of the church who

> ---→
>
> *Challenge your congregation to take risks and watch them rise to the occasion.*
>
> ←---

sits in the seats each weekend. This shift is a major change in the typical pastor's leadership role as well as the congregation's role. Many pastors get comfortable controlling all the ministries of the church, and by doing so, they paralyze the church's growth. We have to trust our congregation with ministries. Do not take all the risks; give some other people a chance to fail. I don't want to be the only one in the church making leadership mistakes. Spread the risk-taking around! Challenge your congregation to take risks and watch them rise to the occasion. In our membership class, for example, people learn not to expect to see me if they are in the hospital, because there is a hospital ministry team. There may be an initial look of shock as your people realize they are the ones who will be doing the ministry. But a confidence level within them results as they see you trust them with ministry.

Multiple Staff

For a church to grow beyond 200, you will have to bring on multiple staff members. This is another contributing factor to the average size of a church in America. The most people one pastor can lead is around 150–200. Therefore, if a church does not have multiple staff, it cannot facilitate growth. Single-staff churches have bottlenecked growth. The Springs was averaging approximately 250 people when we brought on our first full-time worship pastor. We could not afford to pay his salary. Our people caught the vision and gave sacrificially to raise half of his salary before he came on staff.

Recently Teddi and I consulted with Harvest Church, a purpose driven church in Warner Robins, Georgia. The growth had been phenomenal at the church in their first three years. They had met in three different locations and grown to almost 600 people attending on weekends. As we met with them, we quickly realized that the church was seriously understaffed. The pastor, Jim Cowart, and his wife had done an incredible job of leading this rapidly growing church, but they were exhausted. The only full-time staff members were the pastor and his wife. In a meeting with ministry leaders, I explained the rule of thumb for hiring staff—one full-time pastor is needed for each 150 people attending. Immediately the church needed two additional full-time pastoral staff members.

The 150-attendance guideline is logical. Consider that most churches never grow beyond that, or may grow a little beyond 150 and then fall back. This number is the size that one full-time pastor can reasonably manage and control. Remember, a pastor must give up control to allow a church to grow. Not control of the vision, but control of ministries. Pastors must overcome the mindset that they have to visit every person in the hospital, or perform every wedding, or visit everyone who requests a visit. The pastor is not the church; the people are the church. Let the people lead the ministries. This involvement of your people brings a strong level of health to a church, even though it may be uncomfortable at first for the average pastor and church

> ----▶
> *The pastor
> is not the church;
> the people are
> the church.*
> ◀----

member. A strong leader can lead larger than the 150:1 ratio if they give up ministries to laity. My deferment to the people is the reason The Springs grew to 250 before bringing on our second full-time-staff member. Our people carried most of the ministry of the church, and we found the combination of multiple staff members and lay ministry to be a catalyst to explosive growth.

As a church grows beyond 1,000, the ratio of full-time pastors to those in attendance changes. The Springs has seven full-time pastors with 2,500 people attending, a ratio of 343 people to every one pastor. Keep in mind, I am writing about pastors not support staff. A church needs support staff to keep the busywork off the pastors. The constant struggle for a growing church will be hiring enough staff members without going over the salary cap. A healthy rule of thumb is that a church should try to not spend over 50% of the general operating budget for staff salaries and benefits. Once a church gets beyond 50%, the warning light should go on. One megachurch in recent years went far beyond the salary cap with 85% of the operating budget going to staff salaries. The downturn in the economy forced them to cut their budget drastically, and when 85% of your budget is people and the budget is strained, people have to be released.

One difficult issue for churches is determining staff salaries. Many church staff I have encountered are underpaid and overworked. This salary issue can be a touchy subject because no pastor wants to appear to be in ministry for the money. Crooked television preachers have created such a picture of financial opulence and abuse that there is a tendency to swing *far* right of their appeal for money. The financial compensation pendulum has swung too far right in many churches today. Somehow we have equated poverty with humility, and we believe a pastor should be humble. How can a dollar value be placed on any human being's contribution to an organization? But where do we go for guidance on this crucial topic for churches? The best resource I have found is a Compensation Survey from the National Association of Church Business Administrators (NACBA) that they make available on their Web site, *www.nacba.net.* Their survey of thousands of church compensation packages from around the country gives a church hard data from which to make salary decisions. It also takes the pressure off the personnel team who has to annually determine how much their pastor is worth. NACBA gives salary ranges for every position in a church, offering them by size, budget, and region. Most churches are shocked to discover that their salary ranges are out of line. Adequate staff, fairly paid, will be your greatest investment in growing the church.

A church is never actually able to afford additional staff. Have you ever talked to somebody who said, "We're waiting until we can afford to have children before we get pregnant?" Those people do not have children, because they will never be able to afford kids. Likewise, you can never afford additional staff and it will always be a risk. But as your church grows, you must take the plunge and add multiple paid staff members. Every good staff member should pay for themselves in the first six months. They will bring in enough new people to enlarge the church's financial base. If they do not, you probably hired the wrong person. We will talk about that later in the chapter.

Multiple Services

After you have added staff, add additional worship services. Multiple services give people options. We live in the age of choices. Multiple services is a lesson the Protestant Church can learn from the Catholic Church. Catholics have been offering multiple masses for decades. Many churches have locked into the one 11:00 a.m. on Sunday service; however, we must learn how to ask a very important question—why? Why do we only offer one service at 11:00? This service time is left over from farming days when the farmers were able to go out and work the fields in the morning and get to church by 11:00. There are probably not many farmers in your church or community. The point is, every time you add a service you drop another hook in the water.

Do not add a second service too quickly, however. You will need a critical mass in each service to keep it growing. For momentum purposes, the last thing a pastor wants to contend with is going back to one service. That move will cost you leadership points with the church. Timing is everything. In fact, timing is the difference between a home run and a foul ball. A church should consider a second service when the current service is 80% full. When a worship center reaches 80% capacity, you have for the most part, finished growing in that service. At this capacity, people have to search for seats, and guests will not be prone to come back if it is difficult to find a seat. In order for a service to stand on its own, the attendance should be at least 100 people for that service.

The Springs added a Saturday night service when we were three-years old. Attendance was initially pretty strong. We began with around 150 people. Within four months, attendance had fallen to 75 people. We lost momentum and had to punt the Saturday night service. Standing in front of the Saturday group and telling them we were discontinuing the service was painful. I would rather have a root canal than do that again! Saturday services do work, but they take a lot of vision casting to stick. Do not attempt a Saturday night service until you have two healthy Sunday morning services. We have discovered that even unchurched people still think you are supposed to go to church on Sunday morning. When you do begin a Saturday service, sell your heart to it, and make it a win for the people. Tell them that because of tremendous growth "we need your seat on Sunday morning." Then ask half of them to commit to Saturday night for six months to make room for people far from God. Further explain that you need them and are counting on them, then ask them to sign a commitment card signifying their Saturday night commitment. With a short-term commitment, a lot more people will try the service. Over time, some will drift back to Sunday. But many will realize they enjoy having Sundays to themselves. At The Springs, we currently have two Saturday night services and two Sunday morning services. Nearly half of our people go to church on Saturday night.

Adding a second service on Sunday will pay big dividends for your children's ministry. You double your pool of workers for ministry. Ask people to come serve during one service and worship in the other. When there is only one service, the workers in children's ministry do not get to go to church. In that case, many churches offer them a free tape of the service for sacrificing in ministry, a good short-term solution, but it is not healthy for long periods of time. A tape does not replace a worship experience with the body of Christ. Multiple services alleviate this challenge. One additional note: make certain the same ministries are offered during all services. If you are targeting families, make children's ministry available during all services.

As previously stated, as our bodies grow, our skeletal structure must also grow to support the additional size and weight. Similarly, we must restructure the church to accommodate the next level of growth. What structurally worked for 100 people in the first year will not work for 500 people five years later. With every 40% growth an organization experiences, the organizational structure must also be changed. If your structure does not adapt, the church will crumble under the growth.

---

[1] Stanley, Andy, *The Next Generation Leader,* 9.

[2] Tillapaugh, Frank R., *Unleashing the Church: Getting People Out of the Fortress and into Ministry.* (Ventura, Calif.: Regal Books), 1985.

CHAPTER 16

Hiring
Staff

When it comes to hiring church staff, all of us get to experience joys and pains. A good staff will be your greatest joy as a church grows. They will be your partners in ministry, the friends who have invested their lives in the trenches of spiritual combat with you. These will be the ones who cover your back and lift you up in prayer, the ones who understand the direction, vision, and passion of the church. When you hire the right staff, they will be some of your closest friends through the years. Our staff has seen some of the biggest God moments of our lives together in ministry. We have also experienced some of our greatest heartaches together in ministry. We have knocked heads and disagreed on issues as the church has grown, but we have always been committed to the vision of leading our generation to God in Ocala. Over time, God has transformed the staff into a team who does life together. That is staff at its best.

Dream	Design	Launch	Development	Strategic Leadership
0–3 Months	4–6 Months	6–8 Months	8–12 Months	1 Year and Beyond

Unfortunately, the most challenging lessons I have learned came from the pain of poor decisions in hiring staff. I hope some of my mistakes can help you avoid making some of the same mistakes. Proverbs 26:10 (GNT) warns of the pain of poor decisions: *An employer who hires any fool that comes along is only hurting everybody concerned.*

Résumés are the Beginning of the Search, Not the End

Everybody looks great on paper, so do not hire based on a résumé alone. In the interview process, ask the tough questions. As you study a résumé, look for the gaps between dates and get an accounting of the entire work history. Gaps should provide plenty of questions to ask your potential employee, such as, "Where were you during this season?" "What happened between these two staff positions?" Always ask why they left a certain position, or why they want to leave now. Another lesson I have learned is to be wary of someone looking for a position. We have learned to look for people who are not looking for a job, instead look for people who are leading growing ministries and content to continue serving in their current church.

Ask the tough morality questions. "Have you ever been unfaithful?" "Has your spouse ever been unfaithful?" That may seem too personal, but a young church cannot afford to hire staff members who are still nurturing wounds from past sin. If there has been adultery, and they have received counseling, and healing, they will be open to talk about what God has done in their lives. If they are hiding the past, there is a reason they are hiding. Ask the questions.

In addition, the only thing references are good for is getting another reference. Generally, everybody on a reference list is going to give a good reference. That is why they are on the list. Only one time did I have a reference tell me they would not hire that person again. Ask references if they know anyone else you can talk to about the potential employee. Always call previous churches or employers, with the exception of their current church, if they have asked you not to contact them.

Follow the CIA Approach to Hiring

In *Courageous Leadership*, Bill Hybels outlines how to build a dream team. It is difficult to improve on his formula for hiring the right staff. CIA is my own version of Bill's staff selection. It has proven the test of time at The Springs.

"C" is for "chemistry." Chemistry is difficult to measure. It is more about your gut feeling toward an individual in the interview process. If you do not naturally connect with that person, do not hire them. They may be incredibly gifted and seem like the perfect fit for the position, but remember you have to live with them every day when they are staff members. Ken Blanchard, co-author of *The One Minute Manager*, counseled Bill Hybels never to put a person on his team who does not have a positive emotional effect on him the minute that person walks into the office. If you have hired an employee you dread seeing come into your office, you have hired the wrong person. Chemistry is even more important in the start of a church. We must build staff teams that energize each other, not teams that antagonize each other. At The Springs, I love going to work. We have created an office culture that energizes us as a team to stay on task and fulfill the vision of our church.

The "I" is for "integrity." Character flaws could put a young church in a tailspin from which it may not be able to recover. It is always tempting to hire someone with stellar abilities and then think we can do character improvement once they are on staff. As goes the leadership, so goes the church. Aim high in the field of integrity for staff selection. Bill Hybels says, "I have learned that in church work an occasional lapse in competence can be accepted. But lapses in character create problems with far-reaching implications."[1] We have hired staff with character flaws, thinking they would grow and develop—what a mistake! The character flaws were like tentacles on an octopus taking down its prey. They infiltrate all ministry areas touched by this person. Character, both good and bad, is magnified in leadership positions. Know their character.

"A" is for "ability." With strong integrity and team chemistry in place, aim high in ability. Peter Drucker, the renowned management author, said "the people we are looking for are neither unhappy nor unemployed."[2] Search for people within your church or in other churches, who have stellar abilities. In a young church, the staff must wear many hats and play many roles. For example, Jerry Moews was such a find for The Springs. Jerry had served faithfully as a volunteer in various roles, and he felt called to full-time ministry. He was the Bakery Manager of a Sam's Club when we asked him to take a part-time position as Preschool Director. We quickly realized we had a team member. With his administrative gifts, Jerry was someone who could turn chaos into order very quickly. We soon moved him into a full-time children's ministry position, and ultimately to Pastor of Ministries and Missions. Presently, he organizes and leads all of the church's ministries and volunteers. Ability is the one area that can be developed if there is a solid work ethic within the person. God has placed some all-star players within your church; search them out and put them on the field.   – – – ➤

Hire People Who Are Strong Where You Are Weak

Every staff needs a balance of gifts and personalities for effective leadership.

➤ – – –

Our natural tendency is to hire people like us. But in order to build a balanced staff we must search out people who are strong where we are weak. In the interview process, ask the person about their spiritual gifts. God organizes the church around spiritual gifts. Every staff needs a balance of gifts and personalities for effective leadership. Often a senior pastor is weak in administration. He is usually a big picture leader, not detail-oriented. If we hire a bunch of big picture visionaries but no one to handle the administrative aspect, the church is in big trouble. One such church start had a visionary leader and no detail people to mobilize the vision. He saw the vision, but did not know how to get the church from where they were to where they needed to be. The result was a church that imploded in frustration and failure.

The opposite gift package is equally as frustrating—a staff full of administrative strategists. They plan themselves to death, and never move toward the vision. They love talking about the details, but they become paralyzed in administrative processes and choke the adventure out of the church. To balance out the visionaries and administrators, you will also need people with mercy gifts on your staff. Without them, your church will lose its heart and compassion. Search for people to be on the staff who shine where you are dull.

For the most part, when a church is young, we need to hire generalists—people who can do many things well. As the church grows, hire specialists—people who can do one or two things exceptionally. As a church grows, the challenge of shifting roles from generalists to specialists is realized when the generalists' abilities are capped at a certain size. This lid is one of the challenges of growth; some of your staff will not be able to go the distance with you. They become increasingly frustrated because they cannot meet the growing expectations of the position. A position that once required average leadership ability in a church of 200 requires exceptional leadership ability in a church of 1,000.

When Possible, Hire from Within

Growing churches search for staff differently than their conventional counterparts. Since purpose driven churches create a culture that is unique to their target, they tend to have their own language and core values. An increasing trend in growing churches is to hire from within, rather than search outside the church. People naturally rise up in leadership through the ministries of the church.

When you hire from within, you do not have to instruct and implant the vision for the church into new staff, they already understand it. Not only do they understand it, but they love it! That is why they became members of the church and

People naturally rise up in leadership through the ministries of the church.

served in ministry in the first place. We also have the opportunity to know the character and abilities of people from within our church. They have served faithfully and proven themselves. You know their work ethic and have observed their relational skills. Hiring staff from within takes a lot of the guesswork out of the hiring process. Conversely, hiring outside is *always* a gamble. Even when we do our homework and check all the references, the failure rate is always higher with staff brought in than with staff raised up. Sometimes they are good people, they just do not fit your church culture. It is almost like attempting to graft in a foreign body part. Sometimes the body rejects the organ, and occasionally the transplant is successful.

In addition, when you hire from within, sometimes you can hire people part-time before full-time, which is another security step in the hiring process. Take every opportunity afforded you to "test-drive" potential full-time staff members. Under the old hiring process of searching for staff outside the church, this part-time arrangement would be difficult to understand. How could a young church offer to move someone to their area to serve part-time on their staff? The only way that could work is to pay to fly someone in on the weekends, like we did with Jeff Scott in the first year of The Springs. However, when you are hiring from within, being part-time becomes a viable option. And of course, the larger a church becomes, the bigger the resource pool for potential staff members. As The Springs has grown, we have found it easier to find the right staff within our walls. Another interesting trend that occurs is when your people start realizing you are hiring from within, they begin to seek out positions. This realization gives you the chance to teach them to be faithful in the little things, and then they may be entrusted with greater opportunities. The value of ministry leadership is taken to a different level. And when ministry leadership is raised, ministry is increased and lives are impacted for eternity.

---

[1] Hybels, Bill, *Courageous Leadership* (Grand Rapids, Mich.: Zondervan, 2002), 81.

[2] Ibid., 84.

CHAPTER 17

Riding Momentum

For I am the Lord your God, who churns up the sea
so that its waves roar . . .

Isaiah 51:15 (NIV)

In *The Purpose Driven Church*, Rick Warren writes, "Surfing is the art of riding waves that God builds. God makes the waves; surfers just ride them. No surfer tries to create waves. If the waves aren't there, you just don't surf that day! On the other hand, when surfers see a good wave, they make the most of it, even if that means surfing in the middle of a storm."[1]

"Our job as church leaders, like experienced surfers, is to recognize a wave of God's Spirit and ride it. It is not our responsibility to make waves but to recognize how God is working in the world and join him in the endeavor."[2]

Rick has taught thousands of pastors how to surf God's waves of growth and revival in this generation. And it is true that "the more skilled we become in riding waves of growth, the more God sends!"[3] Looking back over The Springs' first eleven years, we learned how to ride the waves of momentum. God sends waves of momentum in a church, allowing us to experience growth and excitement through the incredible energy they bring. These waves can be seasonal, expected in many churches around Easter and Christmas, or they can come from the Holy Spirit as he blows across the waters of your congregation. Each new wave will bring change with it, which will be constant, but that change can also be a new church's best friend. So, learn to sight the waves of momentum coming from a distance and then ride on the crest of every wave. Doing so will allow you to navigate the wave effectively and ride it to the shore of change.

Waves of Momentum in a Church

Life change stories

- - - ➤

We have to allow the church to see *life change.*

◄ - - -

We have to allow the church to *see* life change. This truth occurred to me when we were planning our year-end party in 2001. In the early days, we made a tactical error and had an annual business meeting. The problem is that hardly anyone comes to business meetings, so the result was a poorly attended meeting that allowed thirty to fifty people to approve the annual budget for a church of 1,500 people. As a result, we changed the name and gave it a facelift. Instead of pushing a business meeting, we promoted a year-end party to celebrate everything God had done at The Springs. The results were phenomenal. Attendance skyrocketed to over 500 people, and the atmosphere was charged with excitement.

Our staff planned for a huge celebration. We had cakes made, installed three balloon drops in the ceiling, decorated with balloon arrangements, and had clowns doing face painting for the kids. Our people entered the room anticipating a party, and they *were* the party.

In a church, the biggest challenge with any presentation about finances is that it is measured in dollars and cents, so we had to allow our people to see how their giving impacted lives and eternity. When it came time to present the budget, I shared openly my concern with talking just about dollars. Recognizing the need to show life change, I took a risk. I told our people, "We spent $700,000 last year in our Operating Budget. I have to show you what happened as a result of that expense. If you have given your life to Christ at anytime at The Springs, then, in a minute, when we start the video, I want you to come and join me on the stage."

It was a big risk, because we had at least 500 people sitting out in the worship center, and I had no idea who was out there. What if only one or two people walked up on the stage? My heart beat fast as we began running the video of all the baptisms from the previous year. All of a sudden, people started coming up on stage—those lives who had come to Christ at The Springs. I was not emotionally prepared for that moment. I watched incredulously as people poured onto the stage. They hugged me, cried, and thanked me for changing their lives through The Springs. Many of them were leaders of our church ministries. I had forgotten they had given their lives to Christ at The Springs. They were so intricately woven into the fabric of The Springs, they *were* The Springs. Eventually, I had to turn away to the other side of the stage and regain my composure. I was a wreck! When the video had finished there were more people on the stage than in the worship center seats. That moment was frozen forever in my heart; I looked at our people and asked a simple question.

"Was it worth it? Was it worth spending $700,000 dollars last year to change lives?"

The place erupted.

And I asked, "How many of you are in favor of spending $850,000 to do this again next year?"

People shouted and jumped to their feet in applause. It was unanimous! The budget passed, people were excited, and God was honored. That's a party! Toward the end, the band kicked in with "Can't Stop Talkin' About Everything You've Done," the balloons dropped, and we went out of church celebrating. Now that is a wave of momentum. The air was electric and that was just our year-end business meeting.

A church needs to see those changed lives on a regular basis. Keep stories in front of your people through testimonies. In the early days, we would use live testimonies of people who had come to Christ or experienced victory by walking with Christ. People identify with similar challenges in others' lives and personal stories give people hope. Often times a life change story is more powerful than a dozen sermons. We did a series of messages called *Confronting Our Culture*. One message was "Confronting Our Value of Life," as we addressed abortion. Since abortion is an explosive topic, we wanted to show the heartache of abortion in the lives of people. We had several women in our church who valiantly agreed to share their story of having abortions years before. A videographer in our church edited the stories into one of the most powerful sermons I have ever heard. I introduced the topic, and allowed the stories of our ladies to preach the message. After the video rolled, you could hear a pin drop in the auditorium. I then presented a message of hope. To conclude the message, one of the ladies from the video came up and invited all ladies who had experienced the pain of abortion to a post-abortion Bible study she was leading. That day, twelve women came to her to be part of the study.

We teach our people to recycle their pain because God wants to use past pain to comfort someone's present pain. Healing comes by feeling the pain of others, not by concealing our pain in the past. As 2 Corinthians 1:3–4 (NIV) says,

> *Praise be to the God and Father of our Lord Jesus Christ, the Father of compassion and the God of all comfort, who comforts us in all our troubles, so that we can comfort those in any trouble with the comfort we ourselves have received from God.*

Every time we put a changed life before our church, that person becomes a minister to a new group of people, and the church is encouraged. Life change ultimately shows that the church is working and healthy.

Community events

A community event is another momentum builder that attracts large portions of your community to your church. Easter is a natural season for a church to reach people. Even new churches without a facility can take advantage of this potential season of growth through a community event. Connection Church, pastored by Cole Phillips in Kyle, Texas, used an Easter egg hunt to attract people. They advertised it in the community, and 2,000 people showed up for the event.

Journey Church, in New York City, recognized that only 3% of the people living in the city have children, but many have dogs. So they threw a dog party in Central Park one Saturday afternoon, and hundreds of dogs and owners showed up for the party. The Dog Party has become a community event in which Journey hires a photographer

Once people see you are interested in them and their families, the chances of them stepping in the door of your church greatly increases.

to take pictures of dogs and their owners. They present awards throughout the event, and of course, hand out invitations to the church. Once people see you are interested in them and their families, the chances of them stepping in the door of your church greatly increases. A community event also eliminates the stranger factor. They get to meet the church in a *safe* environment and realize the church is made up of normal people.

Earlier I mentioned The Springs community premier of a VeggieTales® movie. We advertised with direct mail, used radio advertising, and a live remote broadcast on location. We had blow-up rides and slides set up in the parking lot and food vendors serving hamburgers, hotdogs, and cotton candy. We turned the parking lot into a carnival. As the momentum built, we kept selling out shows and having to add more. We sold out five shows and had 2,100 people attend the event. It allowed unchurched people to step inside our facility, and see what we offer for their children. Hundreds of people have since come to The Springs through this one community event.

New facilities

Moving to a new facility can be a huge momentum builder for young churches. Established churches realize this fact when they build new facilities. Most churches experience up to 40% growth by moving into a new building. The Springs consistently saw growth by moving in our early years. Out of necessity, we moved our Sunday morning location eight times in the first eight years. We met in fourteen different locations if you add in our midweek services and youth services. Each time we moved a Sunday location, we added almost 100 new people. However, do not move for the sake of moving. Move on purpose.

Each location change was for a specific reason. Either we outgrew the previous space, or the rent was escalating and not financially feasible, or the lease was not renewed. The key to capturing momentum in a move is the win factor. It has to be a *win* in the eyes of your church. The easiest win is "we have outgrown our current facility." People see growth and are excited. Half of our moves were for this reason. In one move, our rent was escalating and it was no longer a wise financial location for a young church. We had been in a settled location allowing us to leave our equipment set up, and the facility was ours to use throughout the week for offices and practices. But then the rent was raised to $12,000 a month. Obviously, it was time to move. We moved to a local theater and became portable for the first time in years. Our people rallied to a new challenge and momentum again erupted at The Springs.

Set outrageous goals

The most dangerous way to lead a church is with safe, obtainable goals. Daydreaming in school was cause for trouble, and that has carried into our adult lives. However, God wants us to dream with him about the impossible. If a goal is obtainable on our own, we do not need God's help or intervention. Goals are simply statements of your faith, so do not be afraid to set goals.

We did a series called *I Love This Place*, originated by North Point Community Church. I cast a vision for a ten-week series at The Springs and challenged members "to dream with me about a ten-week season where we see 200 people come to Christ, and baptize 100 after the tenth week." As soon as those words left my lips the first time publicly, I thought, *this is scary. What if it doesn't happen?*

People want to be part of something big and impossible, because God created us for adventure.

Verbalizing God-inspired impossible goals starts a wave of momentum in a church. People want to be part of something big and impossible, because God created us for adventure. Our people rallied around that vision and goal. During that time, 200 new people stepped into ministry positions. We took part in a ten-week God-inspired season. The momentum built every week of *I Love This Place*. In ten weeks, we saw over 200 people come to Christ. It was cause for a celebration, so we threw another giant party. In addition to our regular baptistery, we set up an inflatable pool in the worship center for baptisms. That night we celebrated with all of heaven, because the impossible had become possible as we baptized

100 people in one night. Do not ever be afraid to cast impossible God-inspired goals for the church.

Take road trips with key leaders

Vision is more caught than taught. Vision is typically caught in motion, not in meetings. The greatest way for your people to capture a vision is to experience it. Take your key leaders to a place where they can experience the vision ten years down the road. Show them a portrait of the vision painted on the canvas of another church. Enlist your leaders to take a road trip to another church and see what they are doing right. Take them to Saddleback Church or Willow Creek, or North Point, or Fellowship Church, to name a few.

Many churches are leading conferences around the country. Through the years, we have taken most of our staff and groups of our leaders to the *Purpose Driven Church Conference* at Saddleback. Saddleback gave our young church the ability to see what we could be twenty years into the future. In order to capture the vision in the hearts of our leaders, we needed to fly a dozen people across the country. Luther Fortinberry, one of our long-term members came back from the PDC Conference and told me "The Springs is going to be the Saddleback of the East Coast!" He caught the vision for our church reaching the unchurched when he went on that road trip to California. A road trip is expensive for a church, but well worth the investment, because it infuses a nucleus of people with a common vision of the future for the church. That vision is powerful and infectious for the entire church.

> *At the core of riding momentum is the willingness to take ever bigger faith-based risks.*

At the core of riding momentum is the willingness to take ever bigger faith-based risks. Every time we moved to a new location, there was a greater financial commitment. Every time we did a community event, we spent money that was needed somewhere else. God gave us the opportunity and we exercised Hebrews 11:1 (NIV):

> *Now faith is being sure of what we hope for and certain of what we do not see.*

Momentum is a faith-based experience for all churches. As the risks get bigger, either we continue to let God stretch our faith, or we shrink back into comfort and complacency. Do not miss opportunities to ride the waves of momentum in your church. Be confident of this one thing: God is always looking for men and women who will risk everything for him. And when he finds them, he uses them to change their generation. What a privilege, what a calling, what a God.

---

[1] Warren, Rick, *The Purpose Driven Church: Growth Without Compromising Your Message & Mission,* (Grand Rapids, Mich.: Zondervan, 1995), 15.

[2] Ibid., 16.

[3] Ibid., 17.

Appendix

Resources for the Journey

CHURCH PLANTING RESOURCES

BOOKS

Purpose Driven Church: Growing without Compromising Your Message & Mission – Rick Warren

Planting New Churches in a Postmodern Age – Ed Stetzer

Ministry Nuts and Bolts: What They Don't Teach Pastors in Seminary – Aubrey Malphurs

Starting a New Church: The Church Planter's Guide to Success – Ralph Moore

Planting Growing Churches for the 21st Century: A Comprehensive Guide for New Churches and Those Desiring Renewal – Aubrey Malphurs

The Church Planters' Toolkit: A Self-Study Resource Kit for Church Planters and Those Who Supervise Them – Robert E. Logan

Church Planting for a Greater Harvest: A Comprehensive Guide – C. Peter Wagner

The Purpose Driven Life: What on Earth Am I Here For? – Rick Warren

High Definition Living: Bringing Clarity to Your Life's Mission – Ed Young

Can We Do That? Innovative Practices that Will Change the Way You Do Church – Andy Stanley and Ed Young

Doing Church as a Team: The Miracle of Teamwork and How It Transforms Churches – Wayne Cordeiro

Rediscovering Church: The Story and Vision of Willow Creek Community Church – Lynne and Bill Hybels

Courageous Leadership – Bill Hybels

Conspiracy of Kindness: A Refreshing Approach to Sharing the Love of Jesus with Others – Steve Sjogren

101 Ways to Reach Your Community – Steve Sjogren

continued

BOOKS, *continued*

An Unstoppable Force: Daring to Become the Church God Had in Mind – Erwin Raphael McManus

Seizing Your Divine Moment: Dare to Live a Life of Adventure – Erwin Raphael McManus

Leadership by the Book: Tools to Transform Your Workplace – Ken Blanchard, Bill Hybels, and Phil Hodges

Failing Forward: Turning Mistakes into Stepping Stones for Success – John C. Maxwell

Margin/The Overload Syndrome: Leaning to Live Within Your Limits – Richard A. Swenson, M.D.

A Step-by-Step Guide to Church Marketing: Breaking Ground for the Harvest – George Barna

Your Church Can Grow – C. Peter Wagner

User Friendly Churches: What Christians Need to Know About the Churches People Love to Go to – George Barna

Building a Contagious Church: Revolutionizing the Way We View and Do Evangelism – Mark Mittelberg with Contributions by Bill Hybel

Leading Life Changing Small Groups – Bill Donahue

Step By Step: Transitioning Your Sunday School to Small Groups – Hal Mayer

The Life You've Always Wanted: Spiritual Disciplines for Ordinary People – John Ortberg

Like a Rock: Becoming a Person of Character – Andy Stanley

Sacred Pathways: Discovering Your Soul's Path to God – Gary L. Thomas

Out of Their Faces and into Their Shoes: How to Understand Spiritually Lost People and Give Them Directions to God – John Kramp

Your Spiritual Gifts Can Help Your Church Grow: How to Find Your Gifts & Use Them to Bless Others – C. Peter Wagner

Handbook for Multi-Sensory Worship Volume I – Kim Miller and The Ginghamsburg Church Worship Team

Handbook for Multi-Sensory Worship Volume II – Kim Miller and The Ginghamsburg Church Worship Team

Planting New Churches in a Postmodern Age – Ed Stetzer

Dynamic Church Planting: A Complete Handbook – Paul Becker

Beyond Church Growth: Action Plans for Developing a Dynamic Church – Robert E. Logan

Videos That Teach – Doug Fields and Eddie James

Videos That Teach 2 – Doug Fields and Eddie James

Group's Blockbuster Movie Illustrations: Over 160 Clips for Your Ministry! – Bryan Belknap

Blockbuster Movie Illustrations the Sequel: Over 170 All-New Clips for Your Ministry – Bryan Belknap

Movie-Based Illustrations for Preaching & Teaching: 101 Clips to Show or Tell – Craig Brian Larson and Andrew Zahn

More Movie-Based Illustrations for Preaching and Teaching: 101 Clips to Show or Tell – Craig Brian Larson and Lori Quicke

CHURCH WEB SITES

www.saddleback.com

www.thesprings.org

www.gccwired.com

www.nyjourney.com

www.seacoastchurch.org (also www.seacoastchurch.com)

www.clovishills.com

www.fellowshipchurch.com

www.willowcreek.org (also www.willowcreek.com)

www.northpoint.org

www.ginghamsburg.org (also www.ginghamsburg.com)

www.fotw.org

www.mecklenburg.org

www.pointofgrace.org (also www.pointofgrace.com)

www.enewhope.org

www.brookhills.org (also www.brookhills.com)

www.kensingtonchurch.org (also www.kensingtonchurch.com)

continued

www.btbf.org

www.centrepointe.org

www.islandchurch.org

www.crossroadscommunity.net

www.fayettecommunity.org

www.fellowshipoforlando.com

www.flamingoroad.org

www.northheartland.org

www.northstarchurch.org (also www.northstarchurch.com)

www.pantego.org

www.rockharbor.org

www.twincitieschurch.com

www.mosaic.org

www.highlandsfellowship.com

DEMOGRAPHIC WEB SITES

www.namb.net (also www.namb.com)

www.demographicsnow.com

www.link2lead.com

www.census.gov

www.freedemographics.com

www.ethnicharvest.org/regions/regionindex.htm

CHURCH PLANTING WEB SITES

www.newchurches.com

www.topfive.org (also www.churchplanting.com) – *Steve Sjogrens top resources for planters*

www.churchplanting.net

www.churchplants.com

www.leadingedgeministries.org

www.passionforplanting.com

www.a29.org

www.plantachurch.com

www.regalcinemedia.com/meetingsnonprofit.asp

www.newchurches.com

www.mislinks.org/church/chplant.htm
www.newchurchspecialties.org
www.cmtcmultiply.org
www.bradboydston.com/html/church_planting.html
www.easumbandy.com
www.plantingministries.org/
www.imb.org/CPM
www.churchplantingvillage.com/
www.weplantchurches.com/
www.churchplanter.com/
www.outreach.ca/
www.crmnet.org/index.html
www.churchplantingtowin.org
www.newthing.org
www.church-planting.org
www.bradboydston.com/handbook
www.mislinks.org/church/chplant.htm
www.youresource.com
www.nazarenenewchurches.org
www.cpcoaches.com

MESSAGE PREPARATION RESOURCES

www.pastors.com
www.creativepastors.com
www.sermonnotes.com
www.willowcreek.com
www.preachingplus.com
www.northheartland.org
www.northpoint.org
www.highbeam.com
www.twincitieschurch.com
www.bible.org
www.wiredchurches.com
www.ginghamsburgglobal.org
www.barna.org

MEDIA RESOURCES

www.churchplantmedia.com

www.harbingeronline.com

www.lumicon.org

www.textweek.com/movies/themeindex.htm

www.valleysolutionsinc.com

www.e-zekiel.com

www.thedetailsgroup.com

www.ultimatepowerpoint.com

www.projectorpeople.com

www.willowvideo.com (also www.willowcreek.com/servicebuilder/)

www.faithhighway.com

www.mplc.com

www.partingwater.com

www.logodesign.com

www.digitaljuice.com

www.churchmedia.net

MUSIC RESOURCES

www.encouragingmusic.com

www.worshipideas.com

www.olga.net

www.integritymusic.com

www.1christian.net

www.hillsong.com

www.lyricsfreak.com

www.sheetmusicplus.com

www.letitsing.com

www.willowcharts.com (also www.willowcreek.com/servicebuilder/)

www.worship.com

www.worshipmax.com

MAILER RESOURCES

www.mustardseedstudio.com
www.detailsdirect.org
www.thedetailsgroup.com
www.breakthroughchurch.com
www.faithspan.com

BIBLE STUDY SOFTWARE

www.e-sword.net (also www.e-sword.com)– *free Bible study software*
www.logos.com – *Bible study software*
www.quickverse.com – *Bible study software*

OTHER HELPFUL LINKS

www.portablechurch.com – *The premier resource for churches in portable locations.*

www.nacba.net – *National Association of Christian Business Administrators: Salary surveys for churches; an invaluable tool for setting salaries in a growing church.*

www.purposedriven.com – *PurposeDriven® Ministry website*
www.onlinerev.com – *Rev Magazine online*
www.leonardsweet.com – *Leonard Sweet's Resources*
www.injoy.com – *John Maxwell's Leadership Resources*
www.friezeconsulting.com – *A collection of management and administrative resources to assist churches.*

www.family.org – *Focus on the Family's Web site*
www.churchsmart.com
www.churchgrowthsoftware.com – *A simple but efficient church management software for a purpose driven church.*

www.shelbyinc.com – *Church management software for churches, denominational headquarters and related ministries*

www.theamericanchurch.org

GENERAL WEB SITES

www.servantevangelism.com
www.smartleadership.com – *Free leadership resources*
www.ChurchLeaderInsights.com
www.jesusfilm.org/jvpa/ (also www.jesusfilm.com)
www.evangelismtoolbox.com
www.fastcompany.com
www.christianitytoday.com
www.crosswalk.com